WITHDRAWN

ZORA NEALE HURSTON
THE
SANCTIFIED
CHURCH

TURTLE ISLAND   BERKELEY

Earlier versions of some of these articles first appeared in *Negro: An Anthology* (Nancy Cunard, editor) and the *New World Journal.* A special thanks to Robert Hemenway; and the staffs of both the Florida Historical Society and the Archive of American Folklore, Library of Congress for help in locating some of the unpublished articles which appear in this volume. And a final special thanks to Toni Cade Bambara and Everette Hurston, Zora's brother, for bestowing their blessing on this project.

SANCTIFIED CHURCH is published by Turtle Island for the Netzahaulcoyotl Historical Society, a non-profit educational corporation engaged in the multi-cultural study of New World history and literature. For more information, address: Turtle Island, 2845 Buena Vista Way, Berkeley, CA 94708.

ISBN 0-913666-44-0   Trade Paperback

Contents

SOME FORWARD REMARKS

The marker Alice Walker erected at Zora's grave in Eatonville, Fla., in 1973 says:

ZORA NEALE HURSTON
1901   1960
Novelist   Folklorist
GENIUS OF THE SOUTH

Now there was a woman who worked. Waitress, manicurist, librettist, lecturer, secretary/companion, producer, scenarist, domestic, novelist, drama coach, file clerk, storyist, traveloguist, playwright, cook. Fun loving and bodacious, Zora was not playing. "I won't deny myself," she said in answer to various camp spokesmen (yeh, men) running out the party lines—CP, Black Mandarin class ("Negrotarians and the Astorperious set"), race protesters and Bohemians (the litterati and the "niggerati"), ramrod anthropologists—not to mention the stifling political and cultural (un)orthodoxies of the dominant class. The woman just would not behave. She had a mission. Knew what her work in this world was. Pursued it.

The Depression, funding sources dried up, Blacks out of favor, the Renaissance played out. She never skipped a beat. Went right on collecting, maintaining, celebrating the genius of Blacksouth folks. At a time when most writers of the Renaissance theoretically acknowledged that all great art was/is derived from the folk and the folk base—or fecundating matrix, as they say in the trade—was Blacksouth, even as they worked diligently to fashion big city literature and to spruce up their speech, Zora, like Sterling Brown and Langston Hughes and very few others, in practice explored the rich vein and never ever ever cut those critical ties with the "lowly down under." "I mean to wrassle me up a future," she said in the teeth of hard times, "or die trying."

7

She wrassled her up a future. From 1925, when she arrived in New York "like a far-flung watermelon" to cop the illustrious *Opportunity Magazine* literary awards in the short story and play categories, to 1948, when she dropped a stitch and let slip her 4th novel—*Seraph on the Sewanee*, Zora produced over a dozen published stories, 2 original musicals, 1 libretto for a folk opera, several articles on voodoo, several on language and lore, 2 major collections of African-American folklore (tales, raps, stories, songs, jokes, riddles, recipes, remedies, and other wisdoms), 4 novels, and 1 autobiography. She'd traveled throughout the south, the Caribbean, Hollywood, Honduras (in search of a lost Mayan city), collected, lectured, won accolades, got talked about, was plagiarized, and went right on stepping (give or take a falter and stumble caused by ill health and a history of short bread and thin ratios). And the letters, articles, defy-type pieces, and a host of essays that never did get published either because—as in the case of those chapters Lippincott dumped from her autobio *Dust Tracks on the Road*—they were too incendiary, or, as they said in those days, "held opinions irrelevant to an autobiography of a writer," or because, as in the case of those essays contracted by *Saturday Evening Post* who filed them away because they were too raw, or, as they said in those days, "did not advance either the war effort or race relations." Uh hunh. Actually, she was very "careful" as a rule when writing for the "wider American readership," as they say. And saved her more explicit all-hang-out pieces and voice/pitch for articles done in Hoyt Fuller's *Negro Digest*.

And she died trying to get somebody, any damn body, to answer her queries and look at her manuscripts. No up and coming unknown novice begging for a little attention, Zora in the last decade of her life had already earned a degree, had an honorary degree bestowed on her, was the recipient of a Rosenwald fellowship, a Guggenheim research grant, an Anisfeld-Wolk award, and a Howard U distinguished alumni award; she had lectured all over the place and at prestigious university campuses; had published widely and frequently and in very prestigious journals; had been active in the promotion of her books and had a credible sales record; had been a film consultant for Paramount, been a contributing editor for *Negro Digest*. But wouldn't nobody give the woman a play.

She died of a stroke in 1960 at the St. Lucie County Welfare Home in Florida. Someone, figuring there might be some cash-negotiable items among her effects, hosed down the little bonfire made of her papers.

And since then, we've only just begun to pull her work from the ashes. In the 60's and 70's, her/our suppressed classic *Their Eyes Were Watching God* was resurrected on the book shelves and on the campuses. *Dust Tracks, Mules and Men, Jonah's Gourd Vine* followed articles by Alice Walker, Mary Helen Washington, Shirley Anne Williams, Darwin Turner, Rita Dandridge. Feature issues in *Negro Digest* with pieces by June Jordan and others. Master theses, dissertations, MLA papers, the lit bio by Hemenway, Alice Walker's Zora reader *I Love Myself When I'm Laughing and Then Again When I'm Looking Mean and Impressive*. Birthday celebrations around the country on January the 7th. Monologues and one-woman shows, an off Broadway play, a film in progress on her life, work, times. *Tell My Horse* in paperback.

And now, this slim volume of essays that represents perhaps X% of her total output in that genre. And tomorrow? Perhaps some fleet-of-foot with stamina and a road map will gather up for us some of the voluminous papers and tapes in existence—not just those at Yale, Dillard, the Schomberg, the Library of Congress, the Amistad archive, U of Fla. the Moreland-Spingarn Library at Howard, et al, but all those letters, journals, notebooks, manuscripts in the basements and attics, steamer trunks and cedar chests of relatives, colleagues, friends, acquaintances, creditors and sons of creditors asprawl the map. . . . Well, it's more'n a notion.

The pieces "Uncle Monday," "Characteristics of Negro Expression," "Spirituals and Neo-Spirituals," and "Conversions and Visions" were written in the earlier half of her most productive period—the 30's (1926ish to 1936ish; just as we say "the 60's," meaning circa 1954 to 1974 sorta). They were published in 1934 in Nancy Cunard's anthology *The Negro*. That's not Nancy of The Laughing Face (she makes my heart a charcoal burner). That's Nancy of the Cunard shipping line family about whom Salvador Dali was wont to exclaim at one of those flamboyant parties of the period—"The Negro! What do I know about the Negro? Everything! I've met Nancy Cunard." Uh hunh.

"High John de Conquer" was originally published in the October, 1943, issue of *American Mercury*. The magazine had been publishing African-American writers now and then during the Renaissance. And in the early 40's published 6 pieces of Zora's. Some she "spruced up" to support the war effort. In *Negro Digest* she spoke more plainly about the "ass-and-all of Democracy." One of the 6 pieces was a story. Another was a piece that cracked on white folks. And that was the end of that.

"Father Abraham," "Cures and Beliefs," "Mother Catherine," "Daddy Mention" and "The Sanctified Church" are from previously unpublished manuscripts. The figures—Uncle, Daddy, Father, Mother—made brief "appearances" in *Mules and Men,* published in 1935, based on collecting trips she'd made through Florida, Alabama, Tennessee, New Orleans and Georgia. High John, of course, had been on her mind and in her mouth since childhood, as were other folk figures and heroes. "When I pitched headforemost into the world," she writes in her Introduction to *Mules and Men,* "I landed in the crib of Negroness. From the earliest rocking of my cradle, I had known about the capers Brer Rabbit is apt to cut . . . and how the devil always outsmarted God and how that over-noble hero John outsmarted the devil. . . ."

The observations that she presents on music and other stylistics of Blackart practice in worship, the medical arts, and rapping appear as early as 1926 when she wrote some pieces about her hometown in A. Phillip Randolph's paper *The Messenger.* "The Sanctified Church" is of especial interest for those who've looked askance at a Baptist minister's daughter—always messin about with voodoo and hoodoo and stuff. My favorite hands down. Ought to be on the required reading list at all schools of divinity.

The latter five pieces were to have been published in *The Florida Negro,* a volume of works that Zora had a hand in assembling in the late 30's while she was both editor of the American Guide Series and supervisor of "the Negro unit" of the Florida Federal Writers project. Had she not wearied of trying to piece together a living wage and gone off to North Carolina College in Durham to take a salaried post as a drama teacher (where she scandalized her/their name by showing up for class in slacks and a black fedora ace deuce), she might have been able to set a fire under appropriate behinds and get the book to press. Alas.

Hopefully, these essays will whet the reader's appetite and maybe even encourage some to pursue the task aforementioned—to collect more of Zora and make it available. "Uncle Monday" is fairly typical of the tales Zora told at boarding school as a kid; tales of people she'd known or heard about traipsing through the stores and homes of Eatonville. Like the recipes and remedies and vision pieces, they reflect a life-long interest in "alternative," as they say, channels of intelligence and being. "Daddy Mention" is fairly typical of tales told in the jook joints she hung out in on her collecting trips. *Mules and Men* has a wealth of both such tales. The sermons and church pieces, as might be expected from a minister's daughter and a Black-south socialized observer with a perfect-pitch ear, work their way into all of her novels, most especially her first, *Jonah's Gourd Vine*. They represent too a life-long concern with spirituality, most haunt-ingly presented in her masterpiece, *Their Eyes Were Watching God*.

Feels good, this volume. It is always a delight and a blessing to encounter Zora in print. The woman, quite simply, did not play.

Toni Cade Bambara
Atlanta, Ga. 8/10/81

Ms. Bambara is currently working on a 90-minute feature film for WGBH-TV on the life, times, and works of Zora Neale Hurston.

The Sanctified Church

Herbs and Herb Doctors

FATHER ABRAHAM

Henry Abraham was born in Manning, South Carolina, 63 years ago of poor parents who earned their livelihood working on plantations. He received practically no schooling, and spent his time working with his parents. At the age of 24 he married Malvinia Stuke, a childhood sweetheart. He obtained work on a locomotive, and later in a large saw mill as timber cutter.

One day a Negro from Florida named Hamp Miller came to Manning to recruit men to work in a turpentine camp for one Russ Edwards of Lawtey. Miller approached Abraham and some other men with this proposition, offering them higher wages than they were getting. Being a thrifty man and having an eye for business, Abraham consented to go. Taking his wife and his new baby daughter, he arrived in Lawtey to live in the quarters of the turpentine camp. This was 35 years ago. (Little did he know at that time that Fate had a certain niche in life for him to fill, not as a laborer in a turpentine camp, but as the "Hoodoo Doctor of Lawtey.")

Henry Abaham worked hard in the turpentine crops and at odd jobs for 20 years. He raised two children. With the years he grew in the esteem and confidence of his boss until he was given the job of recruiter, considered the plum of all camp jobs.

One day, on a trip to Georgia to enlist men, he promptly succeeded in getting a truck-load of men to come to Florida, but at the last moment the men began to grumble and refused to go. Abraham had a habit of holding two pebbles in his hand which he would rub together as he talked, just as others twist a watch-chain or stroke their chins. Suddenly he had an inspiration; looking steadily at the balky Negroes, he said: "Niggers, you see dese two stones in my han'? Ef you don' git in dat truck right now I'll rub em together an' throw the worstes spell on you you ever done hear about." To his surprise and certainly to his joy the terrified men crowded into the truck and Abraham carried them to their new jobs.

From that time on he became conscious of powers that he had heretofore known nothing about. His fame gradually began to spread as that of a man who could "fix you," or "throw a fix." Years later, after he had saved a little money, Abraham bought a few acres of land and began farming. His health was not very good, and physicians diagnosed his case as Bright's disease and heart trouble. As he walked behind the plow trying to till his land, his wife noticed that every few moments he would stop and rest, always complaining of shortness of breath.

One day as he was plowing under the parching sun, he suddenly stopped, his face bathed in perspiration. Calling his wife he said, "Honey, I jes can' do dis yere work; I has a feelin' God's done called his chile for higher t'ings. Eber sence I been a boy I done had dis yere feelin' but I jes didn' obey. 'Quench not the spirit,' saith de Lord." Throwing down his plow Abraham left the field, never to return to it again as a laborer.

He at once began his holy work. People came to visit him with all sorts of diseases and "spells," and they said he helped them all. At first he set no particular fee, his motto apparently being, "Give what the spirit moves you to give"; yet as time passed and his services grew in demand this motto changed to "The laborer is worthy of his hire."

He traveled through the country-side in his horse and buggy ministering to the sick and spell-bound. As he accumulated money he bought and paid cash for 200 acres of additional land, fenced it, and built six 4-room houses on it, covered with corrugated iron. These housed the families who cultivated his extensive holdings. He paid them $1.50 to $2.00 a day when other employers were paying $.75 cents to $1.00.

Strawberries, string beans and corn were his chief products. He was now known as one of the biggest strawberry planters in Bradford County, and shipped as high as a carload of strawberries to eastern markets a day. Laborers were afraid *not* to work for him; they left any job at his request.

As money continued to pour in, Abraham finally discarded his horse and buggy for a specially built Cadillac which cost $3000, and a de luxe Hudson. Both white and black people visited him, some coming from places as far distant as California and Connecticut.

His method of treatment was as follows: as you entered the house he ascertained your name and how much money you had for him. The money was placed in a large Bible lying on the living room table. Abraham then rubbed the afflicted part of the patient's body with his large hands, while intoning some indescribable oath, the only words of which were comprehensible were the names of the various Prophets. When he finished his incantations, he looked you straight in the eye and assured you that you were well, or would be so after a few more treatments. After this procedure cripples would leave, carrying their crutches in their hands; some who hadn't eaten a decent meal in years were able to devour anything that was placed before them.

Abraham often gave his patients a white muslin packet known as a "Christian letter" to be carried on the person at all times. These letters cost from $5 to $25, and were supposed to bring good luck and ward off evil spells and any form of disaster. To lose the letter meant that one was liable to fall under an evil influence and be tormented. In such a case one must hasten to Abraham to procure another, after paying him the customary fee. He also sold other "good luck" pieces for small sums, for use in "little" cases.

One of his patients, Estella Barber, of Lawtey, has this to say about him: "In 1936 I was suffering with indiges', couldn't eat nor drink. I suffered for two years. Then I went to Father Abraham an' as soon as I got on his porch, chile, all my pains done disappear. He treated me an' I went to him three times; the last time I was cured. Haven't had it sence, an' I kin eat anything. One time I din't think about eating . . . I had high blood pressure and Father Abraham said for me to come an' he could cure that too, but you know I didn' had no money, an' I was skeered to, cause I done hear he talk so rough when you don' had no money. I give him three dollars for curin' de indiges', you know. Yes, suh, Father Abraham was a good man." This seems to be the attitude of most of his patients; he did good but was rough if you brought no money.

After 15 years of this work, Abraham had risen from a poor turpentine worker to one of the wealthiest men, white or black, in Bradford County. During his last illness, in June 1937, his wife insisted on calling a physician. He was reluctant at first, fearing criticism from his patients, but he finally yielded. He healed others; himself he could not heal. Within a week he was dead. His funeral was attended by a throng of both races.

Abraham left his widow and two daughters about $4,000 in cash and $8,000 in real estate; he had suffered heavily from the failure of the Starke bank during the depression. One of his daughters has vowed to carry on his work.

CURES AND BELIEFS

The following list represents certain remedies and beliefs held in common throughout the South by practitioners of the various 'old' religions popular within this region.

Poor Eyesight

Many people bare their ears in the belief that part of the virtue will be transferred from their hearing to their sense of sight.

Whooping Cough

Eat fried crow meat, or drink a tea made of sheep manure.

Fever Blisters

Tie a dried eel skin around the affected area, and leave it there until it falls off from use.

Mumps

Vigorously rub the affected area with the marrow obtained from the jowl of a hog. Sardines are also a good cure. The sardines should be eaten by the patient, and the oil rubbed into the affected parts.

Nose Bleed

Drop a set of keys down your back.

Hiccoughs

Place two brown straws on the 'mould' of the head in the form of a cross.

Headache

Rub table salt onto the 'mould' of the head.

Weak Limbs

If a young child, massage the limbs in greasy dishwater every morning. Also, being buried in the sand for a few hours a day can produce strength, especially for the old and the young.

Night Sweats

A bowl of water secretly placed beneath the head of the sufferer for nine straight nights is thought to effect a cure.

Poor Complexion

Bathe the face in fresh urine every morning before uttering a word to anyone around.

Falling Hair

Ask someone of the opposite sex to comb your hair. Never say 'thank you'. If your hair is too thick, comb it with a fork.

Tuberculosis

Alligator tail, especially prepared, and water that has accumulated in old pine tree stumps, should be given to the patient. Also the meat of fattened dogs killed by stealth. Special 'conjure balls', properly prepared by a favorite doctor are also often used to ward off the disease. Annointing the palms and nostrils with iodoform, turpentine and asafetida are also common practices. Some believe that immunization to all contagious diseases may be obtained by reading the Psalms.

External Ailments

Persons of posthumous birth may cure any of these by simply blowing three times upon the affected area, saying after the first breath 'In the name of the Father', after the second 'And in the name of the Son', and after the third 'And the Holy Ghost, A-men'.

General Afflictions

Visit the corpse of one you have known in life, and who was always pleasantly disposed towards you. While no one is looking whisper the name of the deceased, and kindly request that he take your affliction along with him.

Persons born with cauls, commonly called 'veils', over their eyes are credited with supernatural powers such as healing and being able to see ghosts.

If a house is haunted a piece of new lumber should be nailed in a conspicuous place.

Ghosts hate new things.

Horse shoes are also nailed over the door to ward off evil spirits and bad luck.

It is a common belief that murderers are always harassed by the spirits of their victims and often forced to confess. There are numerous instances of murderers being apprehended by the spirits of their victims.

Ghosts are known to frequent the places where they lived and died.

If you see a ghost coming towards your house, you may regard this as a sign that someone will soon be ill.

If a ghost is seen more than once, and you do not wish to see him again, swear at him, and inquire his business. He will immediately give his reason for the visit, and never trouble you again.

CONCERNING BIRTH

An expectant mother should never be without some old articles of clothing. Too elaborate a preparation, however, will frighten the infant's·spirit, and cause death either at birth or during early infancy.

An expectant mother should never raise her arms above her

head, as this is supposed to tie the navel cord around the neck of the unborn child.

If a little boy shows a liking for the expectant mother prior to birth, a girl will be born, and vice versa.

Babies born on the full of the moon will be larger than those born at other times. Midwives expecting babies at such times should decrease the mother's diet.

Pants hung over the bed at night increase the chances for an easy delivery.

The presence of the child's father at birth will help alleviate the pains of childbirth. Some women wear the husband's hat, or other such men's garments, at the time.

The new mother should be fed a diet of tea and crackers for at least three days after delivery. To eat fish is considered extremely dangerous. Nothing from the inside of an animal, nor an oyster, should be allowed.

No one should step over a baby under one year old, as this is said to stunt its growth.

If when a baby is one month old he is carried around the house by the most estimable friend or relative it will help influence the baby's character.

If a child's fingernails are cut before he is a year old, the child will grow up to be a thief. Hence the fingernails should be bitten off by either the mother, or some other member of the family.

If a child's hair is cut before he is a year old it will affect his speech.

Jeering at a woman in labor is good practice; it is thought that arousing the mother's anger will hasten delivery.

A baby born near midnight will be able to see ghosts.

Sugar should be administered locally to ease the pains of childbirth. One woman who had a particularly easy childbirth told her doctor that all the while she had simply looked out the window, and stared at the stars.

MOTHER CATHERINE

One must go straight out St. Claude below the Industrial Canal and turn south on Flood Street and go almost to the Florida Walk. Looking to the right one sees a large enclosure walled round with a high board fence. A half-dozen flags fly bravely from eminences. A Greek cross tops the chapel. A large American flag flies from the huge tent.

A marsh lies between Flood Street and that flag-flying enclosure, and one must walk. As one approaches, the personality of the place comes out to meet one. No ordinary person created this thing.

At the gate there is a rusty wire sticking out through a hole. That is the bell. But a painted notice on the gate itself reads: "Mother Seal is a holy spirit and must not be disturbed."

One does not go straight into the tent, into the presence of Mother Catherine (Mother Seal). One is conducted into the chapel to pray until the spirit tells her to send for you. A place of barbaric splendor, of banners, of embroideries, of images bought and images created by Mother Catherine herself; of an altar glittering with polished brass and kerosene lamps. There are 365 lamps in this building, but not all are upon the main altar.

The walls and ceilings are decorated throughout in red, white and blue. The ceiling and floor in the room of the Sacred Heart are striped in three colors and the walls are panelled. The panels contain a snake design. The African loves to depict the grace of reptiles.

On a placard: *Speak so you can speak again.*

It would take a volume to describe in detail all of the things in and about this chapel under its Greek cross. But we are summoned by a white-robed saint to the presence.

Mother Catherine holds court in the huge tent. On a raised

platform is her bed, a piano, instruments for a ten-piece orchestra, a huge coffee urn, a wood stove, a heater, chairs and rockers and tables. Backless benches fill the tent.

Catherine of Russia could not have been more impressive upon her throne than was this black Catherine sitting upon an ordinary chair at the edge of the platform within the entrance to the tent. Her face and manner are impressive. There is nothing cheap and theatrical about her. She does things and arranges her dwelling as no occidental would. But it is not for effect. It is for feeling. She might have been the matriarchal ruler of some nomad tribe as she sat there with the blue band about her head like a coronet; a white robe and a gorgeous red cape falling away from her broad shoulders, and a box of shaker salt in her hand like a rod of office. And so it seemed perfectly natural for me to go to my knees upon the gravel floor, and when she signalled me to extend my right hand, palm up for the dab of blessed salt, I hurried to obey because she made me feel that way.

She laid her hand upon my head.

"Daughter why have you come here?"

"Mother, I come seeking knowledge."

"Thank God. Do y'all hear her? She come here lookin for wisdom. Eat de salt, daughter, and get yo mind with God and me. You shall know what you come to find out. I feel you. I felt you while you was sitten in de chapel. Bring her a veil."

The veil was brought and, with a fervent prayer, placed upon my head. I did not tell Mother then that I wanted to write about her. That came much later, after many visits. When I did speak of it she was gracious and let me photograph her and everything behind the walls of her Manger.

I spent two weeks with her, and attended nightly and Sunday services continuously at her tent. Nothing was usual about these meetings. She invariably feeds the gathering. Good, substantial food too. At the Sunday service the big coffee urn was humming, and at a certain point she blessed bread and broke it, and sprinkled on a bit of salt. This she gave to everyone present. To the adults she also gave a cup of coffee. Every cup was personally drawn, sweetened and tasted by her and handed to the communicants as they passed before the platform. At one point she would command everyone to file past the painted barrel and take a glass of water. These things had no inner meaning to an agnostic, but it did drive the dull monotony of the usual Christian service away. It was something, too, to watch the faith it aroused in her followers.

All during her sermons the two parrots were crying from their cages. A white cockatoo would scream when the shouting got too loud. Three canary birds were singing and chirping happily all through the service. Four mongrel dogs strolled about. A donkey, a mother goat with her kid, numbers of hens, a sheep—all wandered in and out of the service without seeming out of place. A Methodist or Baptist church—or one of any denomination whatever—would have been demoralised by any of these animals. Two dogs fought for a place beside the heater. Three children under three years of age played on the platform in the rear without distracting the speaker or the audience. The blue and red robed saint stood immobile in her place directly behind the speaker and the world moved on.

Unlike most religious dictators Mother Catherine does not crush the individual. She encourages originality. There is an air of gaiety about the enclosure. All of the animals are treated with tenderness.

No money is ever solicited within the enclosure of the Manger. If you feel to give, you may. Mother wears a pouch suspended from her girdle. You may approach the platform at any time and drop your contribution in. But you will be just as welcome if you have nothing. All of the persons who live at the Manger are there at Mother Catherine's expense. She encourages music and sees that her juveniles get off to school on time.

There is a catholic flavor about the place, but it is certainly not catholic. She has taken from all the religions she knows anything about any feature that pleases her.

Hear Mother Seal: "Good evening, Veils and Banners!

"God tells me to tell you (invariable opening) that He hold the world in the middle of His hand.

"There is no hell beneath this earth. God wouldn't build a hell to burn His breath.

"There is no heaven beyond dat blue globe. There is a between-world between this brown earth and the blue above. So says the beautiful spirit.

"When we die, where does the breath go? Into trees and grass and animals. Your flesh goes back to mortal earth to fertilize it. So says the beautiful spirit.

"Our brains is trying to make something out of us. Everybody can be something good.

"It is right that a woman should lead. A womb was what God made in the beginning, and out of that womb was born Time, and all that fills up space. So says the beautiful spirit.

"Some are weak to do wisdom things, but strong to do wicked things.

"He could have been born in the biggest White House in the world. But the reason He didn't is that he knowed a falling race was coming what couldn't get to no great White House, so He got born so my people could all reach.

"It is not for people to know the whence.

"Don't teach what the apostles and prophets say. Go to the tree and get the pure sap and find out whether they were right.

"No man has seen spirit—men can see what spirit does, but no man can see spirit."

As she was ready to grant blessings an evil thought reached her and she sat suddenly on a chair and covered her face with her hands, explaining why she did so. When it passed she rose, "Now I will teach you again."

Here the food was offered up but not distributed until the call came from the spirit.

St. Prompt Succor brought the basin and towel at a signal. She washed her hands and face.

It is evident that Mother Seal takes her stand as an equal with Christ.

No nailing or building is done on Friday. A carpenter may saw or measure, but no nailing or joining.

She heals by the laying on of hands, by suggestion and copious doses of castor oil and Epsom salts. She heals in the tent and at great distances.

She has blessed water in the barrel for her followers, but she feels her divinity to such an extent that she blesses the water in the hydrants at the homes of her followers without moving out of her tent.

No one may cross his legs within the Manger. That is an insult to the spirit.

Mother Catherine's conception of the divinity of Christ is that Joseph was his foster father as all men are foster fathers, in that all children are of God and all fathers are merely the means.

All of her followers wear her insignia. The women wear a veil of unbleached muslin; the men, an arm-band. All bear the crescent and M.C.S. (Mother Catherine's Saints) . They must be worn everywhere.

In late February and early March it rained heavily and many feared a flood. Mother Seal exhorted all of her followers to pin their faith in her. All they need do is believe in her and come to her and eat the blessed fish she cooked for them and there would be no flood. "God," she said, "put oars in the fishes hands. Eat this fish and you needn't fear the flood no more than a fish would."

All sympathetic magic. Chicken, beef, lamb are animals of pleasing blood. They are used abundantly as food and often in healing. A freshly killed chicken was split open and bound to a sore leg.

27

All of her followers, white and colored, are her children. She has as many of one race as the other.

"I got all kinds of children, but I am they mother. Some of 'em are saints; some of 'em are conzempts (convicts) and jail-birds; some of 'em kills babies in their bodies; some of 'em walks the streets at night—but they's all my children. God got all kinds, how come I cain't love all of mine? So says the beautiful spirit."

"Now y'all go home in faith. I'm going to appear to you all in three days. Don't doubt me. Go home in faith and pray."

There is a period in the service given over to experiences.

One woman had a vision. She saw a flash of lightning on the wall. It wrote, "Go to Mother Seal." She came with pus on the kidneys and was healed.

A girl of fourteen had a vision of a field of spinach that turned to lilies with one large lily in the middle. The field was her church and the large lily was Mother Catherine.

Most of the testimony has to do with acknowledging that they have been healed by Mother's power, or relating how the wishes they made on Mother came true.

Mother Catherine's religion is matriarchal. Only God and the mother count. Childbirth is the most important element in the creed. Her compound is called the Manger, and is dedicated to the birth of children in or out of wedlock.

Over and over she lauds the bringing forth. *There is no sinful birth.* And the woman who avoids it by abortion is called a "damnable extrate."

Mother Catherine was not converted by anyone. Like Christ, Mohammed, Buddha, the call just came. No one stands between her and God.

After the call she consecrated her body by refraining from the sex relation, and by fasting and prayer.

She was married at the time. Her husband prayed two weeks before he was converted to her faith. Whereupon she baptised him in a tub in the backyard. They lived together six months as holy man and woman before the call of the flesh made him elope with one of her followers.

She held her meetings first on Jackson Avenue, but the crowds that swarmed about her made the authorities harry her. So some of her wealthy followers bought the tract of land below the Industrial Canal where the Manger now is.

God sent her into the Manger over a twelve-foot board fence—not through a gate. She must set no time for her going but when the spirit gave word. After her descent through the roof of the chapel she has never left the grounds but once, and that was not intentional. She was learning to drive a car within the enclosure. It got out of control and tore a hole through the fence before it stopped. She called to her folllowers to "Come git me!" (She must not set her foot on the unhallowed ground outside the Manger.) They came and reverently lifted her and bore her back inside. The spot in the yard upon which she was set down became sacred, for a voice spoke as her feet touched the ground and said, "Put down here the Pool of Gethsemane so that the believers may have holy water to drink." The well is under construction at this writing.

UNCLE MONDAY

People talk a whole lot about Uncle Monday, but they take good pains not to let him hear none of it. Uncle Monday is an out-and-out conjure doctor. That in itself is enough to make the people handle him carefully, but there is something about him that goes past hoodoo. Nobody knows anything about him, and that's a serious matter in a village of less than three hundred souls, especially when a person has lived there for forty years and more.

Nobody knows where he came from nor who his folks might be. Nobody knows for certain just when he did come to town. He was just there one morning when the town awoke. Joe Lindsay was the first to see him. He had some turtle lines set down on Lake Belle. It is a hard lake to fish because it is entirely surrounded by a sooky marsh that is full of leeches and moccasins. There is plenty of deep water once you pole a boat out beyond the line of cypress pines, but there are so many alligators out there that most people don't think the trout are worth the risk. But Joe had baited some turtle lines and thrown them as far as he could without wading into the marsh. So next morning he went as early as he could see light to look after his lines. There was a turtle head on every line, and he pulled them up, cursing the 'gators for robbing his hooks. He says he started on back home, but when he was a few yards from where his lines had been set something made him look back, and he nearly fell dead. For there was an old man walking out of the lake between two cypress trees. The water there was too deep for wading, and besides, he says the man was not wading, he was walking vigorously as if he were on dry land.

Lindsay says he was too scared to stand there and let the man catch up with him, and he was too scared to move his feet; so he just stood there and saw the man cross the marshy strip

30

and come down the path behind him. He says he felt the hair rise on his head as the man got closer to him, and somehow he thought about an alligator slipping up on him. But he says the alligators were in the front of his mind that morning because, first, he had heard bull 'gators fighting and bellowing all night long down in this lake, and then his turtle lines had been robbed. Besides, everybody knows that the father of all 'gators lives in Belle Lake.

The old man was coming straight on, taking short quick steps as if his legs were not long enough for his body, and working his arms in unison. Lindsay says it was all he could do to stand his ground and not let the man see how scared he was, but he managed to stand still anyway. The man came up to him and passed him by without looking. After he had passed, Lindsay noticed that his clothes were perfectly dry, so he decided that his own eyes had fooled him. The old man must have come up to the cypress trees in a boat and then crossed the marsh by stepping from root to root. But when he went to look, he found no convenient roots for anybody to step on. Moreover, there was no boat on the lake either.

The old man looked queer to everybody, but still no one would believe Lindsay's story. They said that he had seen no more than several others—that is, that the old man had been seen coming from the direction of the lake. That was the first that the village saw of him, way back in the late eighties, and so far, nobody knows any more about his past than that. And that worries the town.

Another thing that struck everybody unpleasantly was the fact that he never asked a name nor a direction. Just seemed to know who everybody was, and called each and every one by their right name. Knew where everybody lived too. Didn't earn a living by any of the village methods. He didn't garden, hunt, fish, nor work for the white folks. Stayed so close in the little shack that he had built for himself that sometimes three weeks would pass before the town saw him from one appearance to another.

Joe Clarke was the one who found out his name was Monday. No other name. So the town soon was calling him Uncle Monday. Nobody can say exactly how it came to be known that he was a voodoo man. But it turned out that that was what he was. People said he was a good one too. As much as they feared him, he had plenty of trade. Didn't take him long to take all the important cases away from Aunt Judy, who had had a monopoly for years.

He looked very old when he came to town. Very old, but firm and strong. Never complained of illness.

But once, Emma Lou Pittman went over to his shack early in the morning to see him on business, and ran back with a fearsome tale. She said that she noticed a heavy trail up to his door and across the steps, as if a heavy bloody body had been dragged inside. The door was cracked a little and she could hear a great growling and snapping of mighty jaws. It wasn't exactly a growling either, it was more a subdued howl in a bass tone. She shoved the door a little and peeped inside to see if some varmint was in there attacking Uncle Monday. She figured he might have gone to sleep with the door ajar and a catamount, or a panther, or a bob-cat might have gotten in. He lived near enough to Blue Sink Lake for a 'gator to have come in the house, but she didn't remember ever hearing of them tracking anything but dogs.

But no; no varmint was inside there. The noise she heard was being made by Uncle Monday. He was lying on a pallet of pine straw in such agony that his eyes were glazed over. His right arm was horribly mangled. In fact, it was all but torn away from right below the elbow. The side of his face was terribly torn too. She called him, but he didn't seem to hear her. So she hurried back for some men to come and do something for him. The men came as fast as their legs would bring them, but the house was locked from the outside and there was no answer to their knocking. Mrs. Pittman would have been made out an awful liar if it were not for the trail of blood. So they concluded that Uncle Monday had gotten hurt somehow and had dragged himself home, or had been dragged by a friend. But who could the friend have been?

Nobody saw Uncle Monday for a month after that. Every day or so, someone would drop by to see if hide or hair could be found of him. A full month passed before there was any news. The town had about decided that he had gone away as mysteriously as he had come.

But one evening around dusk-dark Sam Merchant and Jim Gooden were on their way home from a squirrel hunt around Lake Belle. They swore that, as they rounded the lake and approached the footpath that leads towards the village, they saw what they thought was the great 'gator that lives in the lake crawl out of the marsh. Merchant wanted to take a shot at him for his hide and teeth, but Gooden reminded him that they were loaded with bird shot, which would not even penetrate a 'gator's hide, let alone kill it. They said the thing they took for the 'gator then struggled awhile, pulling off something that looked like a long black glove which had come from his right paw. Then without looking either right or left, he stood upright and walked on towards the village. Everybody saw Uncle Monday come thru the town, but still Merchant's tale was hard to swallow. But, by degrees, people came to believe that Uncle Monday could shed any injured member of his body and grow a new one in its place. At any rate, when he reappeared, his right hand and arm bore no scars.

The village is even skeptical about his dying. Once Joe Clarke said to Uncle Monday, "I'god, Uncle Monday, aint you skeered to stay way off by yo'self, old as you is?"

Uncle Monday asked, "Why would I be skeered?"

"Well, you liable to take sick in de night sometime, and you'd be dead befo' anybody would know you was even sick."

Uncle Monday got up off the nail keg and said in a voice so

low that only the men right close to him could hear what he said, "I have been dead for many a year. I have come back from where you are going." Then he walked away with his quick short steps, and his arms bent at the elbow, keeping time with his feet.

It is believed that he has the singing stone, which is the greatest charm, the most powerful "hand" in the world. It is a diamond and comes from the mouth of a serpent (which is thought of as something different from any ordinary snake) and it is the diamond of diamonds. It not only lights your home without the help of any other light, but it also warns its owner of approach.

The serpents who produce these stones live in the deep waters of Lake Maitland. There is a small island in this lake and a rare plant grows there which is the serpent's only food. She comes only to nourish herself in the height of a violent thunderstorm, when she is fairly certain that no human being will be present.

It is impossible to kill or capture her unless nine healthy people have gone before to prepare the way with The Old Ones, and then more will die in the attempt to conquer her. But it is not necessary to kill or take her to get the stone. She has two. One is embedded in her head, and the other she carries in her mouth. The first one cannot be had without killing the serpent, but the second one may be won from her by trickery.

Since she carries this stone in her mouth, she cannot eat until she has put it down. It is her pilot, that warns her of danger. So when she comes upon the island to feed, she always vomits the stone and covers it with earth before she goes to the other side of the island to dine.

To get this diamond, dress yourself all over in black velvet. Your assistant must be dressed in the same way. Have a velvet-covered bowl along. Be on the island before the storm reaches its height, but leave your helper in the boat and warn him to be ready to pick you up and flee at a moment's notice.

Climb a tall tree and wait for the coming of the snake. When she comes out of the water, she will look all about her on the ground to see if anyone is about. When she is satisfied that she is alone, she will vomit the stone, cover it with dirt and proceed to her feeding ground. Then, as soon as you feel certain that she is busy eating, climb down the tree as swiftly as possible, cover the mound hiding the stone with the velvet-lined bowl and flee for your life to the boat. The boatman must fly from the island with all possible speed. For as soon as you approach the stone it will ring like chiming bells, and the serpent will hear it. Then she will run to defend it. She will return to the spot, but the velvet-lined bowl will make it invisible to her. In her wrath she will knock down grown trees and lash the island like a hurricane. Wait till a calm fair day to return for the stone. She never comes up from the bottom of the lake in fair weather. Furthermore, a serpent who has lost her mouth-stone cannot come to feed alone after that. She must bring her mate. The mouth-stone is their guardian, and when they lose it they remain in constant danger unless accompanied by one who has the singing stone.

They say that Uncle Monday has a singing stone, and that is why he knows everything without being told.

Whether he has the stone or not, nobody thinks of doubting his power as a hoodoo man. He is feared, but sought when life becomes too powerful for the powerless. Mary Ella Shaw backed out of Joe-Nathan Moss the day before the wedding was to have come off. Joe-Nathan had even furnished the house and bought rations. His people, her people, everybody tried to make her marry the boy. He loved her so, and besides he had put out so much of his little cash to fix for the marriage. But Mary Ella just wouldn't. She had seen Caddie Brewton, and she was of the kind who couldn't keep her heart still after her eye had already wandered.

So Joe-Nathan's mama went to see Uncle Monday. He said, "Since she is the kind of woman that lets her mind follow her eye, we'll have to let the snake-bite cure itself. You go on home. Never no man will keep her. She kin grab the world full of men, but she'll never keep one any longer than from one full moon to the other."

Fifteen years have passed. Mary Ella has been married four times. She was a very pretty girl, and men just kept coming, but not one man has ever stayed with her longer than the twenty-eight days. Besides her four husbands, no telling how many men she has shacked up with for a few weeks at a time. She has eight children by as many different men, but still no husband.

John Wesley Hogan was another driver of sharp bargains in love. By his own testimony and experience, all women from eight to eighty were his meat, but the woman who was sharp enough to make him marry her wasn't born and her mama was dead. They couldn't frame him and they couldn't scare him.

Mrs. Bradley came to him nevertheless about her Dinkie. She called him out from his work-place and said, "John Wesley, you know I'm a widder woman and I aint got no husband to go to de front for me, so I reckon I got to do de talkin' for me and my chile. I come in de humblest way I know how to ask you to go 'head and marry my chile befo' her name is painted on de signposts of scorn."

If it had not made John Wesley so mad, it would have been funny to him. So he asked her scornfully, "Woman, whut you take me for? You better git outa my face wid dat mess! How you reckon *I* know who Dinkie been foolin round wid? Don't try to come dat mess over *me*. I been all over de North. I ain't none of yo' fool. You must think I'm Big Boy. They kilt Big Boy shootin after Fat Sam so there aint no mo' fools in de world. Ha, ha! All de wimmen *I* done seen! I'll tell you like de monkey tole de elephant—don't bull me, big boy! If you want Dinkie to git married off so bad, go grab one of dese country clowns. I aint yo' man. 'Taint no use you goin running to de high-sheriff neither. I got witness to prove Dinkie knowed more'n I do."

Mrs. Bradley didn't bother with the sheriff. All he could do was to make John Wesley marry Dinkie; but by the time the interview was over that wasn't what the stricken mother wanted. So she waited till dark, and went on over to Uncle Monday.

Everybody says you don't have to explain things to Uncle Monday. Just go there, and you will find that he is ready for you when you arrive. So he set Mrs. Bradley down at a table, facing a huge mirror hung against the wall. She says he had a loaded pistol and a huge dirk lying on the table before her. She looked at both of the weapons, but she could not decide which one she wanted to use. Without a word, he handed her a gourd full of water and she took a swallow. As soon as the water passed over her tongue she seized the gun. He pointed towards the looking-glass. Slowly the form of John Wesley formed in the glass and finally stood as vivid as life before her. She took careful aim and fired. She was amazed that the mirror did not shatter. But there was a loud report, a cloud of bluish smoke and the figure vanished.

On the way home, Brazzle told her that John Wesley had dropped dead, and Mr. Watson had promised to drive over to Orlando in the morning to get him a coffin.

AUNT JUDY BICKERSTAFF

Uncle Monday wasn't the only hoodoo doctor around there. There was Aunt Judy Bickerstaff. She was there before the coming of Uncle Monday. Of course it didn't take long for professional jealousy to arise. Uncle Monday didn't seem to mind Aunt Judy, but she resented him, and she couldn't hide her feelings.

This was natural when you consider that before his coming she used to make all the "hands" around there, but he soon drew off the greater part of the trade.

Year after year this feeling kept up. Every now and then some little incident would accentuate the rivalry. Monday was sitting on top of the heap, but Judy was not without her triumphs.

Finally she began to say that she could reverse anything that he put down. She said she could not only reverse it, she could throw it back on *him*, let alone his client. Nobody talked to him about her boasts. People never talked to him except on business anyway. Perhaps Judy felt safe in boasting for this reason.

Then one day she took it in her head to go fishing. Her children and grandchildren tried to discourage her. They argued with her about her age and her stiff joints. But she had her grandson to fix a trout pole and a bait pole and set out for Blue Sink, a lake said to be bottomless by the villagers. Furthermore, she didn't set out till near sundown. She didn't want any company. It was no use talking, she felt that she just must go fishing in Blue Sink.

She didn't come home when dark came, and her family worried a little. But they reasoned she had probably stopped at one of her friends' houses to rest and gossip so they didn't go to hunt her right away. But when the night wore on and she didn't return, the children were sent out to locate her.

She was not in the village. A party was organized to search Blue Sink for her. It was after nine o'clock at night when the party found her. She was in the lake. Lying in a shallow water and keeping her old head above water by supporting it on her elbow. Her son Ned said that he saw a huge alligator dive away as he shined the torch upon his mother's head.

They bore Aunt Judy home and did everything they could for her. Her legs were limp and useless and she never spoke a word, not a coherent word, for three days. It was more than a week before she could tell how she came to be in the lake.

She said that she hadn't really wanted to go fishing. The

family and the village could witness that she never had fooled around the lakes. But that afternoon she *had* to go. She couldn't say why, but she knew she must go. She baited her hooks and stood waiting for a bite. She was afraid to sit down on the damp ground on account of rheumatism. She got no bites. When she saw the sun setting she wanted to come home, but somehow she just couldn't leave the spot. She was afraid, terrribly afraid down there on the lake, but she couldn't leave.

When the sun was finally gone and it got dark, she says she felt a threatening powerful evil all around her. She was fixed to the spot. A small but powerful whirlwind arose right under her feet. Something terrific struck her and she fell into the water. She tried to climb out, but found that she could not use her legs. She thought of 'gators and otters, and leeches and gar-fish, and began to scream, thinking maybe somebody would hear her and come to her aid.

Suddenly a bar of red light fell across the lake from one side to the other. It looked like a fiery sword. Then she saw Uncle Monday walking across the lake to her along this flaming path. On either side of the red road swam thousands of alligators, like an army behind its general.

The light itself was awful. It was red, but she never had seen any red like it before. It jumped and moved all the time, but always it pointed straight across the lake to where she lay helpless in the water. The lake is nearly a mile wide, but Aunt Judy says Uncle Monday crossed it in less than a minute and stood over her. She closed her eyes from fright, but she saw him right on thru her lids.

After a brief second she screamed again. Then he growled and leaped at her. "Shut up!" he snarled. "Part your lips just one more time and it will be your last breath! Your bragging tongue has brought you here and you are going to stay here until you acknowledge my power. So you can throw back my work, eh? I put you in this lake; show your power and get out. You will not die, and you will not leave this spot until you give consent in your heart that I am your master. Help will come the minute you knuckle under."

She fought against him. She felt that once she was before her own altar she could show him something. He glowered down upon her for a spell and then turned and went back across the lake the way he had come. The light vanished behind his feet. Then a huge alligator slid up beside her where she lay trembling and all her strength went out of her. She lost all confidence in her powers. She began to feel if only she might either die or escape from the horror, she would never touch another charm again. If only she could escape the maw of the monster beside her! Any other death but that. She wished that Uncle Monday would come back so that she might plead with him for deliverance. She opened her mouth to call, but found that speech left her. But she saw a light approaching by land. It was the rescue party.

Aunt Judy never did regain the full use of her legs, but she got to the place where she could hobble about the house and yard. After relating her adventure on Lake Blue Sink she never called the name of Uncle Monday again.

The rest of the village, always careful in that respect, grew almost as careful as she. But sometimes when they would hear the great bull 'gator, that everybody knows lives in Lake Belle, bellowing on cloudy nights, some will point the thumb in the general direction of Uncle Monday's house and whisper, "The Old Boy is visiting the home folks tonight."

Characteristics
of Negro Expression

DADDY MENTION

Just when or where Daddy Mention came into being will require some research; none of the guests at the Blue-Jay seem to know. Only one thing is certain about the wonder-working gentleman: he must have existed, since so many people claim to have known him.

Not that any of his former friends can describe Daddy Mention to you, or even tell you very many close details about him. They agree, however, that he has been an inmate of various and sundry Florida jails, prison camps and road farms for years, and from the stories told of him he must have enjoyed an almost unbroken stay in various places of incarceration.

In fact, it is this unusual power of omnipresence that first arouses the suspicions of the listener; was Daddy Mention perhaps a legendary figure? Prisoners will insist that he was in the Bartow jail on a 90-day sentence, "straight up" when they were doing 60. Then another will contradict and say it must have been some other time, because that was the period when Daddy was in Marion County, "making a bit in the road gang." The vehemence with which both sides argue would seem to prove that Daddy was in neither place, and that very likely he was nowhere.

Legendary though Daddy Mention may be, however, the tales of his exploits are vividly told by the prisoners. All the imagination, the color and the action of the "John Henry" stories cycle are duplicated in Daddy's activities; it is peculiar that the exploits, far-fetched though they may seem, seldom fall on unbelieving ears.

DADDY MENTION'S ESCAPE

"Daddy Mention liked the Polk County jails alright, all except the little jug outside of Lakeland. He told 'em when they put him in there that he didn't think he could stay with them too long.

"They had locked him up for vagrancy, you see. And Daddy Mention didn't think much of that, because jes like he had told them he had been picking oranges, and just had too much money to work for a week or two. He tried to tell them that he would go back to work as soon as he got broke, but you know you can't say much in Polk County.

"So they locked Daddy Mention up; gave him ninety straight up. (Ninety days with no time off for good behavior.) He went on the stump-grubbing gang. Then he got to the Farm.

"It was afternoon when Daddy Mention started to work, and he made the first day allright. He fussed a little, kinda under his breath, when he saw what the prisoners et for supper, but he didn't say much. Then next morning he et breakfast—grits and bacon grease, but no bacon—with the rest of us, and went out to the woods.

"Before it was 10 o'clock—you know you start at 6 in Polk County—Cap'm Smith had cussed at Daddy two or three times; he didn't work fast enough to suit em down there. When we went for dinner he was growlin' at the table: 'Dey ain't treatin' me right.'

"After dinner, when we lined up to go back to the woods, Cap'm Smith walked over to Daddy. 'Boy,' he hollered, 'you gonna work this afternoon, or you want to go to the box?'

"Daddy Mention didn't say nothing at first, then kinda slow he said: 'Whatever you want me to do, Cap'm.'

"Cap'm Smith didn't know what to make of that, and he put Daddy in the box in a hurry. He didn't go back for him that day, neither. He didn't go back till the next day. 'You think you want to come out of there and work, boy?' he asked Daddy Mention, an' Daddy Mention told him again: 'Whatever you want me to do, Cap'm.'

"I didn't see Cap'm Smith then, but they tell me that he got so hot you could fry eggs on him. He slammed the box shut, and didn't go back for Daddy Mention for another day.

"Daddy Mention didn't get out then, though. Every day Cap'm Smith asked him the same thing, and every day Daddy Mention said the same thing.

"Finally Cap'm Smith figured that maybe Daddy Mention wasn't trying to be smart, but was just dumb that way. So one day he let Daddy Mention come out, and let him go with another gang, the tree-chopping gang, working just ahead of us.

"Daddy Mention was glad to get out, 'cause he had made up his mind to go to Tampa. He told some of his gang about it when the Cap'm wasn't listening. But Daddy Mention knew that he couldn't run away, though; you can't do that down there. They'd have you back in jail before you got as far as Mulberry.

"Oh no! Daddy Mention knew he had to have a better plan. And he made one up too. None of us knew much about it, 'cause he didn't talk about it then. But we begin seein' him doing more work than anybody else in the gang; he would chop a tree by hisself, and wouldn't take but one more man to help him lift it to the pile. Then one day, when he was sure his cap'm saw him, he lifted one all by hisself and carried it a long ways before he put it down.

"The Cap'm didn't believe any man could grab one of them big pines and lift it by hisself, much less carry it around. He call Daddy Mention and make him do it again, then he make him do it so the other guards kin see it.

"It wa'n't long before the Cap'm and his friends was picking up a little side money betting other folks that Daddy Mention could pick up any tree they could cut. And they didn't fuss so much when he made a couple of bumpers (nickels) showing off his lifting hisself.

"So it got to be a regular sight to see Daddy Mention walking around the jail yard carrying a big tree in his arms. Everybody was getting used to it by then. That was just what Daddy Mention wanted. One afternoon we came in from the woods, and Daddy Mention was bringing a tree-butt with him. The Cap'm thought one of the other guards musta told him to bring it in, and didn't ask him nothing about it.

"Daddy Mention took his tree-butt to the dining room and stood it up by the wall, then went on with the rest of us and et his dinner. He didn't seem in no hurry or nothing, but he jes didn't have much to say.

"After dinner he waited 'til nearly everybody got finished, then he got up and went back to his log. Most of the Cap'ms an' guards was around the yard then, and all of em watched while Daddy Mention picked up that big log.

"Daddy Mention clowned around in front of the guards for a minute, then started towards the gate with the log on his shoulder. None of the guards didn't bother him, cause who ever saw a man trying to escape with a pine butt on his shoulder?

"You know you have to pass the guard's quarters before you get to the gate in the Lakeland Blue Jay. But Daddy Mention didn't even turn around when he pass, and nobody didn' say nothing to him. The guards musta thought the other guards sent him somewhere with the log, or was making a bet or something.

"Right on out the gate Daddy Mention went, and onto the

road that goes to Hillsborough County. He still had the log on his shoulder. I never saw him again till a long time after, in Tampa. I never did figure out how he got into Hillsborough County from Polk, with watchers all along the road, after he left the Lakeland Blue Jay. So I ask him.

"He say, 'I didn' had no trouble. I jes kep that log on my shoulder, an everybody I pass thought it had fell off a truck, an' I was carrying it back. They knew nobody wouldn' have nerve enough to steal a good pine log like that and walk along with it. They didn' even bother me when I got out of Polk County. But soon's I got to Plant City, though, I took my log to a little woodyard an' sold it. Then I had enough money to RIDE to Tampa. They aint gonna catch me in Polk County no more.'"

DADDY MENTION AND THE MULE

"Daddy Mention git a long trip to Raiford once. Dey wuz a lot of people workin' on de Canal near Ocala, an' they wuz makin' good money. Daddy Mention, he was makin' better money den dey wuz, though. You see, he wa'nt workin' 'xackly on de Canal; he wuz sellin' a little whiskey on the side to dem dat wuz.

"Dey didn' let the Ocala police arres' nobody on de Canal. De county cops didn' bother you much, neither. Dere wuz some special men could bother you, but ef you didn' raise a ruckus, dey wouldn' care.

"But Daddy Mention uster have to go to Ocala whenever his liquor run out. He wuz smaht, though; he uster git one of de white men on de camp t' drive him in an' bring him back. Dat-away de police in Ocala didn' had a chance to git him.

"It uster make de cops mad as a stunned gopher to see Daddy Mention come ridin' right into town wid dis yere white feller, den go ridin' back to de Canal agin, an' dey couldn' git dere han's on him.

"But one time Daddy Mention done jes git his little load o' likker an' dey had started back when de white feller he see somebody he knowed. So he git out o' de truck an' tole Daddy Mention to wait a minute.

"He didn' have to tell him dat; de cop came an' put Daddy Mention where he kin wait a long time, real comfortable. De policeman he wait a long time for a chance to lock Daddy Mention up. So he think he would have a li'le fun wid him. So he stahted pretendin' to joke with Daddy Mention, an' kinnin' him about allus ridin' in to town wid dat white man: 'You mus' t'ink you as good as white folks,' he tole Daddy Mention, an' laugh.

"Daddy Mention he think de cop wuz really playin' wid him, so he stahted tellin' stories. He tole him 'bout how de Lord wuz makin' men, an' put all de dough in de oven. 'He take out de fust dough,' say Daddy, 'an' it wa'nt nowhere near brown; it wuz just yaller. So he set it aside, an' later it become all dem folks what lives in foreign countries, dem Turks an' all. Den He take out a real brown batch uf dough.' Daddy Mention tole de policeman how dis batch look, well-done an' season' jes right. 'Dese wuz de cullud folks,' say Daddy. De policemans dey all laugh; Daddy didn' see dem winkin' at each other.

"'What become of de rest of de dough?' dey ask Daddy. 'Oh dat,' say Daddy, 'dat what wuz lef' over, dey done make all de policemans in de world outa dat.' Den Daddy Mention he laugh as hard as he could, an' de policemans dey laugh too.

"I don' know ef de jedge done laugh, though. He give Daddy Mention two years de nex' day. Dat's how Daddy git to Raiford an' git to know Jinny.

"It take Daddy Mention a long time to figure out he really in de Big Rock for two years or better. When he finally git it through his haid, he begin tellin' folks he wouldn' stay dere no two year.

"You can' beat Cap'm Chapman's Jinny, dey try to tell him. But Daddy Mention he laugh; he ax em how, ef he done drown houn' dogs in de swamp an' done dodge guards wid double-barrell' Winches' kin a mule stop him?

"Lotsa other prisoners dey try to tell Daddy Mention, but he wouldn' have it no other way but he mus' try to escape an' make it to de Okeenokee Swamp up de other side o' Olustee.

"So one mornin', soon as dey let us out in the yard, Daddy Mention ups an' runs. He wuz in good shape, too; he beat dem shot guns a mile.

"When he git a chance to look back over his shoulder he sees one o' de guards put his finger in his mouth and whistle. But didn' no dog come; out come trottin' a li'le, short, jackass-lookin' mule, an' she back' into a li'le drop-bottom cart wid nobody techin' her.

"It don' take but a minute to hitch dat Jinny into dat cart, an' by de time de harness wuz on her all uf de dogs wuz in de bottom uf de cart an' it was flying down de fiel' after Daddy Mention.

"Daddy Mention wuz smaht; he had stole one o' de other prisoner's shoes befo' he lef', so when he git to de woods he take off his shoes an' put on dese. Den he throw his shoes in de ditch, to fool de dogs. An' it done fool em too. Daddy he had time to fin' hisself a good big oak tree an' kivver hisself in it befo' de dogs come an' lost his trail. So he wuz doin' a lot of laughin' to hisself when dey went on across de ditch an' kep' on barkin' an' runnin' furder away. De cart that Jinny wuz pullin' de dogs in wuz standin' a li'le ways off fum his tree too.

"Daddy Mention he wuz busy watchin' de dogs an' figurin' when could he come down and hit it fer de swamp, when he feel somepin grab at his pants. Befo' he kin figure out what is it, it had tore de whole seat out of em, an' maybe a li'le bit of Daddy Mention too. Den he see it wuz Jinny. She have two feets on de bottom of de tree an' wuz reachin' for another piece of Daddy Mention's pants. He try to hurry up a li'le higher, an' one of his feets slip' down a li'le. Dat when Jinny show him she et leather too.

"Daddy, he didn' know what to do. He go round to de other side o' de tree, an' jump down to run. Jinny she come right on behin' him. He have to keep goin' dat same way, cause de dogs wuz still runnin' roun' de other way.

"Befo' Daddy knowed it Jinny had done chase him right back to de prison fence. But he think even gittin' back inside'd be better'n git et up by dat wil' mule, so he lit out fer de top o' de fence. Den jes as he git almos' over, Jinny bit agin. Dis time dere wa'nt no pants for her to bite, so she jes grabbed a mouthful o' Daddy Mention.

"An' dat's where he be when Cap'm Chapman come; right dere, wid a good part o' him in Jinny's mouth. It wuz a long time befo' he kin sit him down to eat. Dat don' worry him so much, cause in de box where he wuz you don' eat much, anyway."

CHARACTERISTICS OF NEGRO EXPRESSION

The Negro's universal mimicry is not so much a thing in itself as an evidence of something that permeates his entire self. And that thing is drama.

His very words are action words. His interpretation of the English language is in terms of pictures. One act described in terms of another. Hence the rich metaphor and simile.

The metaphor is of course very primitive. It is easier to illustrate than it is to explain because action came before speech. Let us make a parallel. Language is like money. In primitive communities actual goods, however bulky, are bartered for what one wants. This finally evolves into coin, the coin being not real wealth but a symbol of wealth. Still later, even coin is abandoned for legal tender, and still later cheques for certain usages.

Every phase of Negro life is highly dramatized. No matter how joyful or how sad the case there is sufficient poise for drama. Everything is acted out. Unconsciously for the most part of course. There is an impromptu ceremony always ready for every hour of life. No little moment passes unadorned.

Now the people with highly developed languages have words for detached ideas. That is legal tender. "That-which-we-squat-on" has become "chair." "Groan-causer" has evolved into "spear" and so on. Some individuals even conceive of the equivalent of cheque words, like "ideation" and "pleonastic." Perhaps we might say that *Paradise Lost* and *Sartor Resartus* are written in cheque words.

The primitive man exchanges descriptive words. His terms are all close fitting. Frequently the Negro, even with detached words in his vocabulary—not evolved in him but transplanted on his tongue by contact—must add action to it to make it do.

49

So we have "chop-axe," "sitting-chair," "cook-pot" and the like because the speaker has in his mind the picture of the object in use. Action. Everything illustrated. So we can say the white man thinks in a written language and the Negro thinks in hieroglyphics.

A bit of Negro drama familiar to all is the frequent meeting of two opponents who threaten to do atrocious murder one upon the other.

Who has not observed a robust young Negro chap posing upon a street corner, possessed of nothing but his clothing, his strength, and his youth? Does he bear himself like a pauper? No, Louis XIV could be no more insolent in his assurance. His eyes say plainly "Female, halt!" His posture exults "Ah, female, I am the eternal male, the giver of life. Behold in my hot flesh all the delights of this world. Salute me, I am strength." All this with a languid posture, there is no mistaking his meaning.

A Negro girl strolls past the corner lounger. Her whole body panging* and posing. A slight shoulder movement that calls attention to her bust, that is all of a dare. A hippy undulation below the waist that is a sheaf of promises tied with conscious power. She is acting out "I'm a darned sweet woman and you know it."

These little plays by strolling players are acted out daily in a dozen streets in a thousand cities, and no one ever mistakes the meaning.

WILL TO ADORN

The will to adorn is the second most notable characteristic in Negro expression. Perhaps his ideas of ornament does not attempt to meet conventional standards, but it satisfies the soul of its creator.

---

*From "pang."

In this respect the American Negro has done wonders to the English language. This is true, but it is equally true that he has made over a great part of the tongue to his liking and has his revision accepted by the ruling class. No one listening to a Southern white man talk could deny this. Not only has he softened and toned down strongly consonanted words like "aren't" to "ain't" and the like, he has made new force words out of old feeble elements. Examples of this are "ham-shanked," "battle-hammed," "double-teen," "bodaciously," "muffle-jawed."

But the Negro's greatest contribution to the language is: (1) the use of metaphor and simile; (2) the use of the double descriptive; (3) the use of verbal nouns.

1. Metaphor and Simile

One at a time, like lawyers going
to heaven.
You sho is propaganda.
Sobbing hearted.
I'll beat you till: (a) rope like okra,
(b) slack like lime, (c) smell like
onions.
Fatal for naked.
Kyting along.
That's a rope.
Cloakers—deceivers.
Regular as pig-tracks.
Mule blood—black molasses.
Syndicating—gossiping.
Flambeaux—cheap cafe (lighted by flambeaux).
To put yo'self on de ladder.

2. The Double Descriptive

High-tall.
Little-tee-ninchy (tiny).
Low-down.
Top-superior.
Sham-polish.
Lady-people.
Kill-dead.
Hot-boiling.
Chop-axe.
Sitting-chairs.
De watch wall.
Speedy-hurry.
More great and more better.

3. Verbal Nouns

She features somebody I know.
Funeralize.
Sense me into it.
Puts the shamery on him.
'Taint everybody you kin confidence.
I wouldn't friend with her.
Jooking—playing piano or guitar as
it is done in Jook-houses (houses of
ill-fame).
Uglying away.
I wouldn't scorn my name all up on you.
Bookooing (beaucoup) around—showing off.

Nouns from Verbs

Won't stand a broke.
She won't take a listen.
He won't stand straightening.
That is such a compliment.
That's a lynch.

The stark, trimmed phrases of the Occident seem too bare for the voluptuous child of the sun, hence the adornment. It arises out of the same impulse as the wearing of jewelry and the making of sculpture—the urge to adorn.

On the walls of the homes of the average Negro one always finds a glut of gaudy calendars, wall pockets and advertising lithographs. The sophisticated white man or Negro would tolerate none of these, even if they bore a likeness to the Mona Lisa. No commercial art for decoration. Neither the calendar nor the advertisement spoils the picture for this lowly man. He sees the beauty in spite of the declaration of the Portland Cement Works or the butcher's announcement. I saw in Mobile a room in which there was an over-stuffed mohair living-room suite, an imitation mahogany bed and chifferobe, a console victrola. The walls were gaily papered with Sunday supplements of the *Mobile Register*. There were seven calendars and three wall pockets. One of them was decorated with a lace doily. The mantel-shelf was covered with a scarf of deep home-made lace, looped up with a huge bow of pink crepe paper. Over the door was a huge lithograph showing the Treaty of Versailles being signed with a Waterman fountain pen.

It was grotesque, yes. But it indicated a desire for beauty. And decorating a decoration, as in the case of the doily on the gaudy wall pocket, did not seem out of place to the hostess. The feeling back of such an act is that there can never be enough of beauty, let alone too much. Perhaps she is right. We each have our standards of art, and thus we are all interested parties and so unfit to pass judgment upon the art concepts of others.

Whatever the Negro does of his own volition he embellishes. His religious service is for the greater part excellent prose poetry. Both prayers and sermons are tooled and polished until they are true works of art. The supplication is forgotten in the frenzy of creation. The prayer of the white man is considered humorous in its bleakness. The beauty of the Old Testament does not exceed that of a Negro prayer.

ANGULARITY

After adornment the next most striking manifestation of the Negro is Angularity. Everything that he touches becomes angular. In all African sculpture and doctrine of any sort we find the same thing.

Anyone watching Negro dancers will be struck by the same phenomenon. Every posture is another angle. Pleasing, yes. But an effect achieved by the very means which a European strives to avoid.

The pictures on the walls are hung at deep angles. Furniture is always set at an angle. I have instances of a piece of furniture in the *middle* of a wall being set with one end nearer the wall than the other to avoid the simple straight line.

ASYMMETRY

Asymmetry is a definite feature of Negro art. I have no samples of true Negro painting unless we count the African shields, but the sculpture and carvings are full of this beauty and lack of symmetry. It is present in the literature, both prose and verse. I offer an example of this quality in verse from Langston Hughes:

> I ain't gonna mistreat ma good gal any more,
> I'm just gonna kill her next time she makes me sore.

I treats her kind but she don't do me right,
She fights and quarrels most every night.

I can't have no woman's got such low-down ways
Cause de blue gum woman aint de style now'days.

I brought her from the South and she's goin on back,
Else I'll use her head for a carpet tack.

It is the lack of symmetry which makes Negro dancing so difficult for white dancers to learn. The abrupt and unexpected changes. The frequent change of key and time are evidences of this quality in music (Note the St. Louis Blues).

The dancing of the justly famous Bo-Jangles and Snake Hips are excellent examples.

The presence of rhythm and lack of symmetry are paradoxical, but there they are. Both are present to a marked degree. There is always rhythm, but it is the rhythm of segments. Each unit has a rhythm of its own, but when the whole is assembled it is lacking in symmetry. But easily workable to a Negro who is accustomed to the break in going from one part to another, so that he adjusts himself to the new tempo.

DANCING

Negro dancing is dynamic suggestion. No matter how violent it may appear to the beholder, every posture gives the impression that the dancer will do much more. For example, the performer flexes one knee sharply, assumes a ferocious face mask, thrusts the upper part of the body forward with clenched fists, elbows taut as in hard running or grasping a thrusting blade. That is all. But the spectator himself adds the picture of ferocious assault, hears the drums and finds himself keeping time with the music and tensing himself for the struggle. It is compelling insinuation. That is the very reason the spectator is held so rapt. He is participating in the performance himself—carrying out the suggestions of the performer.

The difference in the two arts is: the white dancer attempts to express fully; the Negro is restrained, but succeeds in gripping the beholder by forcing him to finish the action the performer suggests. Since no art can ever express all the variations conceivable, the Negro must be considered the greater artist, his dancing is realistic suggestion, and that is about all a great artist can do.

NEGRO FOLKLORE

Negro folklore is not a thing of the past. It is still in the making. Its great variety shows the adaptability of the black man: nothing is too old or too new, domestic or foreign, high or low, for his use. God and the Devil are paired, and are treated no more reverently than Rockefeller and Ford. Both of these men are prominent in folklore. Ford being particularly strong, and they talk and act like good-natured stevedores or mill-hands. Ole Massa is sometimes a smart man and often a fool. The automobile is ranged alongside of the oxcart. The angels and the apostles walk and talk like section hands. And through it all walks Jack, the greatest culture hero of the South; Jack beats them all—even the Devil, who is often smarter than God.

Culture Heroes

The Devil is next after Jack as a culture hero. He can outsmart everyone but Jack. God is absolutely no match for him. He is good-natured and full of humour. The sort of person one may count on to help out in any difficulty.

Peter the Apostle is third in importance. One need not look far for the explanation. The Negro is not a Christian really. The primitive gods are not deities of too subtle inner reflection; they are hard-working bodies who serve their devotees just as laboriously as the suppliant serves them. Gods of physical violence, stopping at nothing to serve their followers. Now of all the apostles, Peter is the most active. When the other ten fell back trembling in the garden, Peter wielded the blade on the posse. Peter first and foremost in all action. The gods of no peoples have been philosophic until the people themselves have approached that state.

The rabbit, the bear, the lion, the buzzard, the fox are culture heroes from the animal world. The rabbit is far in the lead of all the others and is blood brother to Jack. In short, the trickster-hero of West Africa has been transplanted to America.

John Henry is a culture hero in song, but no more so than Stacker Lee, Smokey Joe or Bad Lazarus. There are many, many Negroes who have never heard of any of the song heroes, but none who do not know John (Jack) and the rabbit.

Examples of Folklore and the Modern Culture Hero

Why de Porpoise's Tail is on Crosswise

Now, I want to tell you 'bout de porpoise. God had done made de world and everything. He set de moon and de stars in de sky. He got de fishes of de sea, and de fowls of de air completed. He made de sun and hung it up. Then He made a nice gold track for it to run on. Then He said, "Now, Sun, I got everything made but Time. That's up to you. I want you to start out and go round de world on dis track just as fast as you kin make it. And de time it takes you to go and come, I'm going to call day and night." De Sun went zoomin' on cross de elements. Now, de porpoise was hanging round there and heard God what he told de Sun, so he decided he'd take dat trip round de world hisself. He looked up and saw de Sun kytin' along, so he lit out too, him and dat Sun!

So de porpoise beat de Sun round de world by one hour and

three minutes. So God said, "Aw naw, this aint gointer do! I didn't mean for nothin' to be faster than de Sun!" So God run dat porpoise for three days before he runs him down and caught him, and took his tail off and put it crossways to slow him up. Still he's de fastest thing in de water. And dat's why de porpoise got his tail on crossways.

Rockefeller and Ford

Once John D. Rockefeller and Henry Ford was woofing at each other. Rockefeller told Henry Ford he could build a solid gold road round the world. Henry Ford told him if he would he would look at it and see if he liked it, and if he did he would buy it and put one of his tin lizzies on it.

ORIGINALITY

It has been said so often that the Negro is lacking in originality that it has almost become a gospel. Outward signs seem to bear this out. But if one looks closely its falsity is immediately evident.

It is obvious that to get back to original sources is much too difficult for any group to claim very much as a certainty. What we really mean by originality is the modification of ideas. The most ardent admirer of the great Shakespeare cannot claim first source even for him. It is his treatment of the borrowed material.

So if we look at it squarely, the Negro is a very original being. While he lives and moves in the midst of a white civilization, everything that he touches is re-interpreted for his own use. He has modified the language, mode of food preparation, practice of medicine, and most certainly the religion of his new country, just as he adapted to suit himself the Sheik haircut made famous by Rudolph Valentino.

Everyone is familiar with the Negro's modification of the whites' musical instruments, so that his interpretation has been adopted by the white man himself and then re-interpreted. In so many words, Paul Whiteman is giving an imitation of a Negro orchestra making use of white-invented musical instruments in a Negro way. Thus has arisen a new art in the civilized world, and thus has our so-called civilization come. The exchange and re-exchange of ideas between groups.

IMITATION

The Negro, the world over, is famous as a mimic. But this in no way damages his standing as an original. Mimicry is an art in itself. If it is not, then all art must fall by the same blow that strikes it down. When sculpture, painting, dancing, litera-ture neither reflect nor suggest anything in nature or human ex-perience we turn away with a dull wonder in our hearts at why the thing was done. Moreover, the contention that the Negro imitates from a feeling of inferiority is incorrect. He mimics for the love of it. The group of Negroes who slavishly imitate is small. The average Negro glories in his ways. The highly educat-ed Negro the same. The self-despisement lies in a middle class who scorns to do or be anything Negro. "That's just like a Nig-ger" is the most terrible rebuke one can lay upon this kind. He wears drab clothing, sits through a boresome church service, pre-tends to have no interest in the community, holds beauty con-tests, and otherwise apes all the mediocrities of the white brother. The truly cultured Negro scorns him, and the Negro "farthest down" is too busy "spreading his junk" in his own way to see or care. He likes his own things best. Even the group who are not Negroes but belong to the "sixth race," buy such records as "Shake dat thing" and "Tight lak dat." They really enjoy hear-ing a good bible-beater preach, but wild horses could drag no such admission from them. Their ready-made expression is: "We done got away from all that now." Some refuse to countenance

Negro music on the grounds that it is niggerism, and for that reason should be done away with. Roland Hayes was thoroughly denounced for singing spirituals until he was accepted by white audiences. Langston Hughes is not considered a poet by this group because he writes of the man in the ditch, who is more numerous and real among us than any other.

But, this group aside, let us say that the art of mimicry is better developed in the Negro than in other racial groups. He does it as the mocking-bird does it, for the love of it, and not because he wishes to be like the one imitated. I saw a group of small Negro boys imitating a cat defecating and the subsequent toilet of the cat. It was very realistic, and they enjoyed it as much as if they had been imitating a coronation ceremony. The dances are full of imitations of various animals. The buzzard lope, walking the dog, the pig's hind legs, holding the mule, elephant squat, pigeon's wing, falling off the log, seabord (imitation of an engine starting) , and the like.

ABSENCE OF THE CONCEPT OF PRIVACY

It is said that Negroes keep nothing secret, that they have no reserve. This ought not to seem strange when one considers that we are an outdoor people accustomed to communal life. Add this to all-permeating drama and you have the explanation.

There is no privacy in an African village. Loves, fights, possessions are, to misquote Woodrow Wilson, "Open disagreements openly arrived at." The community is given the benefit of a good fight as well as a good wedding. An audience is a necessary part of any drama. We merely go with nature rather than against it.

Discord is more natural than accord. If we accept the doctrine of the survival of the fittest there are more fighting honors than there are honors for other achievements. Humanity places premiums on all things necessary to its well-being, and a valiant and good fighter is valuable in any community. So why hide the light under a bushel? Moreover, intimidation is a recognized part of warfare the world over, and threats certainly must be listed under that head. So that a great threatener must certainly be considered an aid to the fighting machine. So then if a man or woman is a facile hurler of threats, why should he or she not show their wares to the community? Hence, the holding of all quarrels and fights in the open. One relieves one's pent-up anger and at the same time earns laurels in intimidation. Besides, one does the community a service. There is nothing so exhilarating as watching well-matched opponents go into action. The entire world likes action, for that matter. Hence prize-fighters become millionaires.

Likewise love-making is a biological necessity the world over and an art among Negroes. So that a man or woman who is proficient sees no reason why the fact should not be moot. He swaggers. She struts hippily about. Songs are built on the power to charm beneath the bed-clothes. Here again we have individuals striving to excel in what the community considers an art. Then if all of his world is seeking a great lover, why should he not speak right out loud?

It is all in a view-point. Love-making and fighting in all their branches are high arts, other things are arts among groups where they brag about their proficiency just as brazenly as we do about these things that others consider matters for conversation behind closed doors. At any rate, the white man is despised by Negroes as a very poor fighter individually, and a very poor lover. One Negro, speaking of white men, said, "White folks is alright when dey gits in de bank and on de law bench, but dey sho' kin lie about wimmen folks."

I pressed him to explain. "Well you see, white mens makes out they marries wimmen to look at they eyes, and they know they gits em for just what us gits em for. 'Nother thing, white mens say they goes clear round de world and wins all de wimmen folks way from they men folks. Dat's a lie too. They don't win nothin, they buys em. Now de way I figgers it, if a woman don't want me enough to be wid me, 'thout I got to pay her, she kin rock right on, but these here white men don't know what to do wid a woman when they gits her—dat's how come they gives they wimmen so much. They got to. Us wimmen works jus as hard as us does an come home an sleep wid us every night. They own wouldn't do it and its de mens fault. Dese white men done fooled theyself bout dese wimmen.

"Now me, I keeps me some wimmens all de time. Dat's whut dey wuz put here for—us mens to use. Dat's right now, Miss. Y'll wuz put here so us mens could have some pleasure. Course I don't run round like heap uh men folks. But if my ole lady go way from me and stay more'n two weeks, I got to git me somebody, ain't I?"

Jook is the word for a Negro pleasure house. It may mean a bawdy house. It may mean the house set apart on public works where the men and women dance, drink and gamble. Often it is a combination of all these.

In past generations the music was furnished by "boxes," another word for guitars. One guitar was enough for a dance; to have two was considered excellent. Where two were playing one man played the lead and the other seconded him. The first player was "picking" and the second was "framming," that is, playing chords while the lead carried the melody by dexterous finger work. Sometimes a third player was added, and he played a tom-tom effect on the low strings. Believe it or not, this is excellent dance music.

Pianos soon came to take the place of the boxes, and now player-pianos and victrolas are in all of the Jooks.

Musically speaking, the Jook is the most important place in America. For in its smelly, shoddy confines has been born the secular music known as blues, and on blues has been founded jazz. The singing and playing in the true Negro style is called "jooking."

The songs grow by incremental repetition as they travel from mouth to mouth and from Jook to Jook for years before they reach outside ears. Hence the great variety of subject-matter in each song.

The Negro dances circulated over the world were also conceived inside the Jooks. They too make the round of Jooks and public works before going into the outside world.

In this respect it is interesting to mention the Black Bottom. I have read several false accounts of its origin and name. One writer claimed that it got its name from the black sticky mud on the bottom of the Mississippi River. Other equally absurd statements gummed the press. Now the dance really originated in the Jook section of Nashville, Tennessee, around Fourth Avenue. This is a tough neighborhood known as Black Bottom—hence the name.

The Charleston is perhaps forty years old and was danced up and down the Atlantic seaboard from North Carolina to Key West, Florida.

The Negro social dance is slow and sensuous. The idea in the Jook is to gain sensation, and not so much exercise. So that just enough foot movement is added to keep the dancers on the floor. A tremendous sex stimulation is gained from this. But who is trying to avoid it? The man, the woman, the time and place have met. Rather, little intimate names are indulged in to heap fire on fire.

These too have spread to all the world.

The Negro theatre, as built up by the Negro, is based on Jook situations, with women, gambling, fighting and drinking. Shows like "Dixie to Broadway" are only Negro in cast, and could just as well have come from pre-Soviet Russia.

Another interesting thing—Negro shows before being tampered with did not specialize in octoroon chorus girls. The girl who could hoist a Jook song from her belly and lam it against the front door of the theatre was the lead, even if she were as black as the hinges of hell. The question was "Can she jook?" She must also have a good belly wobble, and her hips must, to quote a popular work song, "Shake like jelly all over and be so broad, Lawd, Lawd, and be so broad." So that the bleached chorus is the result of a white demand and not the Negro's.

The woman in the Jook may be nappy headed and black, but if she is a good lover she gets there just the same. A favorite Jook song of the past has this to say:
Singer: It aint good looks dat takes you through dis world.
Audience: What is it, good mama?
Singer: Elgin* movements in your hips. Twenty years guarantee.
And it always brought down the house too.

> Oh de white gal rides in a Cadillac,
> De yaller girl rides de same,
> Black gal rides in a rusty Ford
> But she gits dere just de same.

The sort of woman her men idealize is 'the type put forth in the theatre. The art-creating Negro prefers a not too thin woman who can shake like jelly all over as she dances and sings, and that is the type he put forth on the stage. She has been banished by the white producer and the Negro who takes his cue from the white.

Of course a black woman is never the wife of the upper class Negro in the North. This state of affairs does not obtain in the South, however. I have noted numerous cases where the wife was considerably darker than the husband. People of some substance, too.

This scornful attitude towards black women receives mouth sanction by the mud-sills.

Even on the works and in the Jooks the black man sings

---

*Elegant (?). [from the Elgin Watch, Ed.]

disparagingly of black women. They say that she is evil. That she sleeps with her fists doubled up and ready for action. All over they are making a little drama of waking up a yaller* wife and a black one.

A man is lying beside his yaller wife and wakes her up. She says to him, "Darling, do you know what I was dreaming when you woke me up?" He says, "No honey, what was you dreaming?" She says, "I dreamt I had done cooked you a big fine dinner and we was setting down to eat out de same plate and I was setting on yo' lap jus huggin you and kissin you and you was so sweet."

Wake up a black woman, and before you kin git any sense into her she be done up and lammed you over the head four or five times. When you git her quiet she'll say, "Nigger, know whut I was dreamin when you woke me up?"

You say, "No honey, what was you dreamin?" She says, "I dreamt you shook yo' rusty fist under my nose and I split yo' head open wid a axe."

But in spite of disparaging fictitious drama, in real life the black girl is drawing on his account at the commissary. Down in the Cypress Swamp as he swings his axe he chants:

Dat ole black gal, she keeps on grumblin,
New pair shoes, new pair shoes,
I'm goint to buy her shoes and stockings
Slippers too, slippers too.

Then adds aside: "Blacker de berry, sweeter de juice."

To be sure the black gal is still in power, men are still cutting and shooting their way to her pillow. To the queen of the Jook!

Speaking of the influence of the Jook, I noted that Mae West in "Sex" had much more flavor of the turpentine quarters than she did of the white bawd. I know that the piece she played

---

*Yaller (yellow), light mulatto

on the piano is a very old Jook composition. "Honey let yo' drawers hang low" had been played and sung in every Jook in the South for at least thirty-five years. It has always puzzled me why she thought it likely to be played in a Canadian bawdy house.

Speaking of the use of Negro material by white performers, it is astonishing that so many are trying it, and I have never seen one yet entirely realistic. They often have all the elements of the song, dance, or expression, but they are misplaced or distorted by the accent falling on the wrong element. Everyone seems to think that the Negro is easily imitated when nothing is further from the truth. Without exception I wonder why the black-face comedians *are* black-face; it is a puzzle—good comedians, but darn poor niggers. Gershwin and the other "Negro" rhapsodists come under this same axe. Just about as Negro as caviar or Ann Pennington's athletic Black Bottom. When the Negroes who knew the Black Bottom in its cradle saw the Broadway version they asked each other, "Is you learnt dat *new* Black Bottom yet?" Proof that it was not *their* dance.

And God only knows what the world has suffered from the white damsels who try to sing Blues.

The Negroes themselves have sinned also in this respect. In spite of the goings up and down on the earth, from the original Fisk Jubilee Singers down to the present, there has been no genuine presentation of Negro songs to white audiences. The spirituals that have been sung around the world are Negroid to be sure, but so full of musicians' tricks that Negro congregations are highly entertained when they hear their old songs so changed. They never use the new style songs, and these are never heard unless perchance some daughter or son has been off to college and returns with one of the old songs with its face lifted, so to speak.

I am of the opinion that this trick style of delivery was originated by the Fisk Singers; Tuskegee and Hampton followed suit and have helped spread this misconception of Negro spirituals. This Glee Club style has gone on so long and become so fixed among concert singers that it is considered quite authentic. But I say again, that not one concert singer in the world is singing the songs as the Negro songmakers sing them.

If anyone wishes to prove the truth of this let him step into some unfashionable Negro church and hear for himself.

To those who want to institute the Negro theatre, let me say it is already established. It is lacking in wealth, so it is not seen in the high places. A creature with a white head and Negro feet struts the Metropolitan boards. The real Negro theatre is in the Jooks and the cabarets. Self-conscious individuals may turn away the eye and say, "Let us search elsewhere for our dramatic art." Let 'em search. They certainly won't find it. Butter Beans and Susie, Bo-Jangles and Snake Hips are the only performers of the real Negro school it has ever been my pleasure to behold in New York.

DIALECT

If we are to believe the majority of writers of Negro dialect and the burnt-cork artists, Negro speech is a weird thing, full of "ams" and "Ises." Fortunately, we don't have to believe them. We may go directly to the Negro and let him speak for himself.

I know that I run the risk of being damned as an infidel for declaring that nowhere can be found the Negro who asks "am it?" nor yet his brother who announces "Ise uh gwinter." He exists only for a certain type of writers and performers.

Very few Negroes, educated or not, use a clear clipped "I." It verges more or less upon "Ah." I think the lip form is responsible for this to a great extent. By experiment the reader will find that a sharp "i" is very much easier with a thin taut lip than with a full soft lip. Like tightening violin strings.

If one listens closely one will note too that a word is slurred in one position in the sentence but clearly pronounced in another. This is particularly true of the pronouns. A pronoun as a subject is likely to be clearly enunciated, but slurred as an object. For example: "You better not let me ketch yuh."

There is a tendency in some localities to add the "h" to "it" and pronounce it "hit." Probably a vestige of Old English. In some localities "if" is "ef."

In story telling "so" is universally the connective. It is used even as an introductory word, at the very beginning of a story. In religious expression "and" is used. The trend in stories is to state conclusions; in religion, to enumerate.

I am mentioning only the most general rules in dialect because there are so many quirks that belong only to certain localities that nothing less than a volume would be adequate.

HIGH JOHN DE CONQUER

High John de Conquer came to be a man, and a mighty man at that. But he was not a natural man in the beginning. First off, he was a whisper, a will to hope, a wish to find something worthy of laughter and song. Then the whisper put on flesh. His footsteps sounded across the world in a low but musical rhythm as if the world he walked on was a singing-drum. Black people had an irresistible impulse to laugh. High John de Conquer was a man in full, and had come to live and work on the plantations, and all the slave folks knew him in the flesh.

The sign of this man was a laugh, and his singing-symbol was a drum-beat. No parading drum-shout like soldiers out for show. It did not call to the feet of those who were fixed to hear it. It was an inside thing to live by. It was sure to be heard when and where the work was the hardest, and the lot the most cruel. It helped the slaves endure. They knew that something better was coming. So they laughed in the face of things and sang, "I'm so glad! Trouble don't last always." And the white people who heard them were struck dumb that they could laugh. In an outside way, this was Old Massa's fun, so what was Old Cuffy laughing for?

Old Massa couldn't know, of course, but High John de Conquer was there walking his plantation like a natural man. He was treading the sweat-flavored clods of the plantation, crushing out his drum tunes, and giving out secret laughter. He walked on the winds and moved fast. Maybe he was in Texas when the lash fell on a slave in Alabama, but before the blood was dry on the back he was there. A faint pulsing of a drum like a goat-skin stretched over a heart, that came nearer and closer, then somebody in the saddened quarters would feel like laughing, and say, "Now, High John de Conquer, Old Massa couldn't get the best of *him*. That old John was a case!" Then everybody sat up and began to smile. Yes, yes, that was right. Old John, High John could beat the unbeatable. He was top-superior to the whole mess of sorrow. He could beat it all, and what made it so cool, finish it off with a laugh. So they pulled the covers up over their souls and kept them from all hurt, harm and danger and made them a laugh and a song. Night time was a joke, because daybreak was on the way. Distance and the impossible had no power over High John de Conquer.

He had come from Africa. He came walking on the waves of sound. Then he took on flesh after he got here. The sea captains of ships knew that they brought slaves in their ships. They knew about those black bodies huddled down there in the middle passage, being hauled across the waters to helplessness. John de Conquer was walking the very winds that filled the sails of the ships. He followed over them like the albatross.

It is no accident that High John de Conquer has evaded the ears of white people. They were not supposed to know. You can't know what folks won't tell you. If they, the white people, heard some scraps, they could not understand because they had nothing to hear things like that with. They were not looking for any hope in those days, and it was not much of a strain for them to find something to laugh over. Old John would have been out of place for them.

Old Massa met our hope-bringer all right, but when Old Massa met him, he was not going by his right name. He was traveling, and touristing around the plantations as the laugh-provoking Brer Rabbit. So Old Massa and Old Miss and their young ones laughed with and at Brer Rabbit and wished him well. And all the time, there was High John de Conquer playing his tricks of making a way out of no-way. .Hitting a straight lick with a crooked stick. Winning the jack pot with no other stake but a laugh. Fighting a mighty battle without outside-showing force, and winning his war from within. Really winning in a permanent way, for he was winning with the soul of the black man whole and free. So he could use it afterwards. For what shall it profit a man if he gain the whole world, and lose his own soul? You would have nothing but a cruel, vengeful, grasping monster come to power. John de Conquer was a bottom-fish. He was deep. He had the wisdom tooth of the East in his head. Way over there, where the sun rises a day ahead of time, they say that Heaven arms with love and laughter those it does not wish to see destroyed. He who carries his heart in his sword must perish. So says the ultimate law. High John de Conquer knew a lot of things like that. He who wins from within is in the "Be" class. *Be* here when the ruthless man comes and *be* here when he is gone.

Moreover, John knew that it is written where it cannot be erased, that nothing shall live on human flesh and prosper. Old Maker said that before He made any more sayings. Even a man-eating tiger and lion can teach a person that much. His flabby muscles and mangy hide can teach an emperor right from wrong. If the emperor would only listen.

II

There is no established picture of what sort of looking-man this John de Conquer was. To some, he was a big, physical-looking man like John Henry. To others, he was a little, hammered-down, low-built man like the Devil's doll-baby. Some said that they never heard what he looked like. Nobody told them, but he lived on the plantation where their old folks were slaves. He is not so well known to the present generation of colored people in the same way that he was in slavery time. Like King Arthur of England, he has served his people, and gone back into mystery again. And, like King Arthur, he is not dead. He waits to return when his people shall call again. Symbolic of English power, Arthur came out of the water, and with Excalibur, went back into the water again. High John de Conquer went back to Africa, but

71

he left his power here, and placed his American dwelling in the root of a certain plant. Possess that root, and he can be summoned at any time.

"Of course, High John de Conquer got plenty power!" Aunt Shady Anne Sutton bristled at me when I asked her about him. She took her pipe out of her mouth and stared at me out of her deeply wrinkled face. "I hope you ain't one of these here smart colored folks that done got so they don't believe nothing, and come here questionizing me so you can have something to poke fun at. Done got shamed of the things that brought us through. Make out 'taint no such thing no more."

When I assured her that that was not the case, she went on.

"Sho John de Conquer means power. That's bound to be so. He come to teach and tell us. God don't leave nobody ignorant, you child. Don't care where He drops you down. He puts you on a notice. He don't want folks taken advantage of because they don't know. Now, back there in slavery time, us didn't have no power of protection, and God knowed it, and put us under watchcare. Rattlesnakes never bit no colored folks until four years after freedom was declared. That was to give us time to learn and to know. 'Course, I don't know nothing about slavery personal like. I wasn't born till two years after the Big Surrender. Then I wasn't nothing but a infant baby when I was born, so I couldn't know nothing but what they told me. My mama told me, and I know she wouldn't mislead me, how High John de Conquer helped us out. He had done teached the black folks so they knowed a hundred years ahead of time that freedom was coming. Long before the white folks knowed anything about it at all.

"These young Negroes reads they books and talk about the war freeing the Negroes, but Aye, Lord! A heap sees, but a few knows. 'Course, the war was a lot of help, but how come the war took place? They think they knows, but they don't. John de Conquer had done put it into the white folks to give us our freedom, that's what. Old Massa fought against it, but us could have told him that it wasn't no use. Freedom just *had* to come. The time set aside for it was there. That war was just a sign and a symbol of the thing. That's the truth! If I tell the truth about everything as good as I do about that, I can go straight to Heaven without a prayer."

Aunt Shady Anne was giving the inside feeling and meaning to the outside laughs around John de Conquer. He romps, he clowns, and looks ridiculous, but if you will, you can read something deeper behind it all. He is loping on off from the Tar Baby with a laugh.

Take, for instance, those words he had with Old Massa about stealing pigs.

Old John was working in Old Massa's house that time, serving around the eating table. Old Massa loved roasted young pigs, and had them often for dinner. Old John loved them too, but Massa never allowed the slaves to eat any at all. Even put aside the left-over and ate it next time. John de Conquer got tired of that. He took to stopping by the pig pen when he had a strong taste for pig-meat, and getting himself one, and taking it on down to his cabin and cooking it.

Massa began to miss his pigs, and made up his mind to squat for who was taking them and give whoever it was a good hiding. So John kept on taking pigs, and one night Massa walked him down. He stood out there in the dark and saw John kill the pig and went on back to the "big house" and waited till he figured John had it dressed and cooking. Then he went on down to the quarters and knocked on John's door.

"Who dat?" John called out big and bold, because he never dreamed that it was Massa rapping.

"It's me, John," Massa told him. "I want to come in."

"What you want, Massa? I'm coming right out."

"You needn't to do that, John. I want to come in."

"Naw, naw, Massa. You don't want to come into no old

slave cabin. Youse too fine a man for that. It would hurt my feelings to see you in a place like this here one."

"I tell you I want to come in, John!"

So John had to open the door and let Massa in. John had seasoned that pig *down,* and it was stinking pretty! John knowed Old Massa couldn't help but smell it. Massa talked on about the crops and hound dogs and one thing and another, and the pot with the pig in it was hanging over the fire in the chimney and kicking up. The smell got better and better.

Way after while, when that pig had done simbled down to a low gravy, Massa said, "John, what's that you cooking in that pot?"

"Nothing but a little old weasly possum, Massa. Sickliest little old possum I ever did see. But I thought I'd cook him anyhow."

"Get a plate and give me some of it, John. I'm hungry.

"Aw, naw, Massa, you ain't hongry."

"Now, John, I don't mean to argue with you another minute. You give me some of that in the pot, or I mean to have the hide off of your back tomorrow morning. Give it to me!"

So John got up and went and got a plate and a fork and went to the pot. He lifted the lid and looked at Massa and told him, "Well, Massa, I put this thing in here a possum, but if it comes out a pig, it ain't no fault of mine."

Old Massa didn't want to laugh, but he did before he caught himself. He took the plate of brownded-down pig and ate it up. He never said nothing, but he gave John and all the other house servants roast pig at the big house after that.

III

John had numerous scrapes and tight squeezes, but he usually came out like Brer Rabbit. Pretty occasionally, though, Old Massa won the hand. The curious thing about this is, that there are no bitter tragic tales at all. When Old Massa won, the thing ended up in a laugh just the same. Laughter at the expense of the slave, but laughter right on. A sort of recognition that life is not one-sided. A sense of humor that said, "We are just as ridiculous as anybody else. We can be wrong, too."

There are many tales, and variants of each, of how the Negro got his freedom through High John de Conquer. The best one deals with a plantation where the work was hard, and Old Massa mean. Even Old Miss used to pull her maids' ears with hot fire-tongs when they got her riled. So, naturally, Old John de Conquer was around that plantation a lot.

"What we need is a song," he told the people after he had figured the whole thing out. "It ain't here, and it ain't no place I knows of as yet. Us better go hunt around. This has got to be a particular piece of singing."

But the slaves were scared to leave. They knew what Old Massa did for any slave caught running off.

"Oh, Old Massa don't need to know you gone from here. How? Just leave your old work-tired bodies around for him to look at, and he'll never realize youse way off somewhere, going about your business."

At first they wouldn't hear to John, that is, some of them. But, finally, the weak gave in to the strong, and John told them to get ready to go while he went off to get something for them to ride on. They were all gathered up under a big hickory nut tree. It was noon time and they were knocked off from chopping cotton to eat their dinner. And then that tree was right where Old Massa and Old Miss could see from the cool veranda of the big house. And both of them were sitting out there to watch.

"Wait a minute, John. Where we going to get something to wear off like that. We can't go nowhere like you talking about dressed like we is."

"Oh, you got plenty things to wear. Just reach inside your-selves and get out all those fine raiments you been toting around with you for the last longest. They is in there, all right. I know. Get 'em out, and put 'em on."

So the people began to dress. And then John hollered back for them to get out their musical instruments so they could play music on the way. They were right inside where they got their fine raiments from. So they began to get them out. Nobody remembered that Massa and Miss were setting up there on the veranda looking things over. So John went off for a minute. After that they all heard a big sing of wings. It was John come back, riding on a great black crow. The crow was so big that one wing rested on the morning, while the other dusted off the evening star.

John lighted down and helped them, so they all mounted on, and the bird took out straight across the deep blue sea. But it was a pearly blue, like ten squillion big pearl jewels dissolved in running gold. The shore around it was all grainy gold itself.

Like Jason in search of the golden fleece, John and his party went to many places, and had numerous adventures. They stopped off in Hell where John, under the name of Jack, married the Devil's youngest daughter and became a popular character. So much so, that when he and the Devil had some words because John turned the dampers down in old Original Hell and put some of the Devil's hogs to barbecue over the coals, John ran for High Chief Devil and won the election. The rest of his party was overjoyed at the possession of power and wanted to stay there. But John said no. He reminded them that they had come in search of a song. A song that would whip Old Massa's earlaps down. The song was not in Hell. They must go on.

The party escaped out of Hell behind the Devil's two fast horses. One of them was named Hallowed-Be-Thy-Name, and the other, Thy-Kingdom-Come. They made it to the mountain. Somebody told them that the Golden Stairs went up from there. John decided that since they were in the vicinity, they might as well visit Heaven.

They got there a little weary and timid. But the gates swung wide for them, and they went in. They were bathed, robed, and given new and shining instruments to play on. Guitars of gold, and drums, and cymbals and wind-singing instruments. They walked up Amen Avenue, and down Hallelujah Street, and found with delight that Amen Avenue was tuned to sing bass and alto. The west end was deep bass, and the east end alto. Hallelujah Street was tuned for tenor and soprano, and the two promenades met right in front of the throne and made harmony by themselves. You could make any tune you wanted to by the way you walked. John and his party had a very good time at that and other things. Finally, by the way they acted and did, Old Maker called them up before His great work-bench, and made them a tune and put it in their mouths. It had no words. It was a tune that you could bend and shape in most any way you wanted to fit the words and feelings that you had. They learned it and began to sing.

Just about that time a loud rough voice hollered, "You Tunk! You July! You Aunt Diskie!" Then Heaven went black before their eyes and they couldn't see a thing until they saw the hickory nut tree over their heads again. There was everything just like they had left it, with Old Massa and Old Miss sitting on the veranda, and Massa was doing the hollering.

"You all are taking a mighty long time for dinner," Massa said. "Get up from there and get on back to the field. I mean for you to finish chopping that cotton today if it takes all night long. I got something else, harder than that, for you to do tomorrow. Get a move on you!"

They heard what Massa said, and they felt bad right off. But John de Conquer took and told them, saying, "Don't pay what he say no mind. You know where you got something finer than this plantation and anything it's got on it, put away. Ain't that funny? Us got all that, and he don't know nothing at all about it. Don't tell him nothing. Nobody don't have to know where us gets our pleasure from. Come on. Pick up your hoes and let's go."

They all began to laugh and grabbed up their hoes and started out.

"Ain't that funny?" Aunt Diskie laughed and hugged herself with secret laughter. "Us got all the advantage, and Old Massa think he got us tied!"

The crowd broke out singing as they went off to work. The day didn't seem hot like it had before. Their gift song came back into their memories in pieces, and they sang about glittering new robes and harps, and the work flew.

IV

So after a while, freedom came. Therefore High John de Conquer has not walked the winds of America for seventy-five years now. His people had their freedom, their laugh and their song. They have traded it to the other Americans for things they could use like education and property, and acceptance. High John knew that that was the way it would be, so he could retire with his secret smile into the soil of the South and wait.

The thousands upon thousands of humble people who still believe in him, that is, in the power of love and laughter to win by their subtle power, do John reverence by getting the root of the plant in which he has taken up his secret dwelling, and "dressing" it with perfume, and keeping it on their person, or in their houses in a secret place. It is there to help them overcome things they feel that they could not beat otherwise, and to bring them the laugh of the day. John will never forsake the weak and the helpless, nor fail to bring hope to the hopeless. That is what they believe, and so they do not worry. They go on and laugh and sing. Things are bound to come out right tomorrow. That is the secret of black song and laughter.

The Sanctified Church

SPIRITUALS AND NEO-SPIRITUALS

The real spirituals are not really just songs. They are unceasing variations around a theme.

Contrary to popular belief their creation is not confined to the slavery period. Like the folk-tales, the spirituals are being made and forgotten every day. There is this difference: the makers of the songs of the present go about from town to town and church to church singing their songs. Some are printed and called ballads, and offered for sale after the services at ten and fifteen cents each. Others just go about singing them in competition with other religious minstrels. The lifting of the collection is the time for the song battles. Quite a bit of rivalry develops.

These songs, even the printed ones, do not remain long in their original form. Every congregation that takes it up alters it considerably. For instance, *The Dying Bed Maker,* which is easily the most popular of the recent compositions, has been changed to *He's a Mind Regulator* by a Baptist church in New Orleans.

The idea that the whole body of spirituals are "sorrow songs" is ridiculous. They cover a wide range of subjects from a peeve at gossipers to Death and Judgment.

The nearest thing to a description one can reach is that they are Negro religious songs, sung by a group, and a group bent on expression of feelings and not on sound effects.

There never has been a presentation of genuine Negro spirituals to any audience anywhere. What is being sung by the concert artists and glee clubs are the works of Negro composers or adaptors *based* on the spirituals. Under this head come the works of Harry T. Burleigh, Rosamond Johnson, Lawrence Brown, Nathaniel Dett, Hall Johnson and Work. All good work and beautiful, but *not* the spirituals. These neo-spirituals are the outgrowth of the glee clubs. Fisk University boasts perhaps the oldest and certainly the most famous of these. They have spread their interpretation over America and Europe. Hampton and Tuskegee have not been unheard. But with all the glee clubs and soloists, there has not been one genuine spiritual presented.

To begin with, Negro spirituals are not solo or quartette material. The jagged harmony is what makes it, and it ceases to be what it was when this is absent. Neither 'can any group be trained to reproduce it. Its truth dies under training like flowers under hot water. The harmony of the true spiritual is not regular. The dissonances are important and not to be ironed out by the trained musician. The various parts break in at any old time. Falsetto often takes the place of regular voices for short periods. Keys change. Moreover, each singing of the piece is a new creation. The congregation is bound by no rules. No two times singing is alike, so that we must consider the rendition of a song not as a final thing, but as a mood. It won't be the same thing next Sunday.

Negro songs to be heard truly must be sung by a group, and a group bent on expression of feelings and not on sound effects.

Glee clubs and concert singers put on their tuxedos, bow prettily to the audience, get the pitch and burst into magnificent song—but not *Negro* song. The real Negro singer cares nothing about pitch. The first notes just burst out and the rest of the church join in—fired by the same inner urge. Every man trying to express himself through song. Every man for himself. Hence the harmony and disharmony, the shifting keys and broken time that make up the spiritual.

I have noticed that whenever an untampered-with congregation attempts the renovated spirituals, the people grow self-conscious. They sing sheepishly in unison. None of the glorious individualistic flights that make up their own songs. Perhaps they feel on strange ground. Like the unlettered parent before his child just home from college. At any rate they are not very popular.

This is no condemnation of the neo-spirituals. They are a valuable contribution to the music and literature of the world. But let no one imagine that they are the songs of the people, as sung by them.

The lack of dialect in the religious expression—particularly in the prayers—will seem irregular.

The truth is, that the religious service is a conscious art expression. The artist is consciously creating—carefully choosing every syllable and every breath. The dialect breaks through only when the speaker has reached the emotional pitch where he loses all self-consciousness.

In the mouth of the Negro the English language loses its stiffness, yet conveys its meaning accurately. "The booming bounderries of this whirling world" conveys just as accurate a picture as mere "boundaries," and a little music is gained besides. "The rim bones of nothing" is just as truthful as "limitless space."

Negro singing and formal speech are breathy. The audible breathing is part of the performance and various devices are resorted to to adorn the breath taking. Even the lack of breath is embellished with syllables. This is, of course, the very antithesis of white vocal art. European singing is considered good when each syllable floats out on a column of air, seeming not to have any mechanics at all. Breathing must be hidden. Negro song ornaments both the song and the mechanics. It is said of a popular preacher, "He's got a good straining voice." I will make a parable to illustrate the difference between Negro and European.

A white man built a house. So he got it built and he told the man: "Plaster it good so that nobody can see the beams and uprights." So he did. Then he had it papered with beautiful paper, and painted the outside. And a Negro built him a house. So when he got the beams and all in, he carved beautiful grotesques over all the sills and stanchions, and beams and rafters. So both went to live in their houses and were happy.

The well-known "ha!" of the Negro preacher is a breathing device. It is the tail end of the expulsion just before inhalation. Instead of permitting the breath to drain out, when the wind gets too low for words, the remnant is expelled violently. Example: (inhalation) "And oh!"; (full breath) "my Father and my wonder-working God"; (explosive exhalation) "ha!"

Chants and hums are not used indiscriminately as it would appear to a casual listener. They have a definite place and time. They are used to "bear up" the speaker. As Mama Jane of Second Zion Baptist Church, New Orleans, explained to me: "What point they come out on, you bear 'em up."

For instance, if the preacher should say: "Jesus will lead us," the congregation would bear him up with: "I'm got my ha-hands in my Jesus' hands." If in prayer or sermon, the mention is made of nailing Christ to the cross: "Didn't Calvary tremble when they nailed him down."

There is no definite post-prayer chant. One may follow, however, because of intense emotion. A song immediately follows prayer. There is a pre-prayer hum which depends for its material upon the song just sung. It is usually a pianissimo continuation of the song without words. If some of the people use the words it is done so indistinctly that they would be hard to catch by a person unfamiliar with the song.

As indefinite as hums sound, they also are formal and can be found unchanged all over the South. The Negroised white hymns are not exactly sung. They are converted into a barbaric chant that is not a chant. It is a sort of liquefying of words. These songs are always used at funerals and on any solemn occasion. The Negro has created no songs for death and burials, in spite of the sombre subject matter contained in some of the spirituals. Negro songs are one and all based on a dance-possible rhythm. The heavy interpretations have been added by the more cultured singers. So for funerals fitting white hymns are used.

Beneath the seeming informality of religious worship there is a set formality. Sermons, prayers, moans and testimonies have their definite forms. The individual may hang as many new ornaments upon the traditional form as he likes, but the audience would be disagreeably surprised if the form were abandoned. Any new and original elaboration is welcomed, however, and this brings out the fact that all religious expression among Negroes is regarded as art, and ability is recognized as definitely as in any other art. The beautiful prayer receives the acolade as well as the beautiful song. It is merely a form of expression which people generally are not accustomed to think of as art. Nothing outside of the Old Testament is as rich in figure as a Negro prayer. Some instances are unsurpassed anywhere in literature.

There is a lively rivalry in the technical artistry of all of these fields. It is a special honor to be called upon to pray over the covered communion table, for the greatest prayer-artist present is chosen by the pastor for this, a lively something spreads over the church as he kneels, and the "bearing up" hum precedes him. It continues sometimes through the introduction, but ceases as he makes the complimentary salutation to the deity. This consists in giving to God all the titles that form allows.

The introduction to the prayer usually consists of one or two verses of some well-known hymn. "O, that I knew a secret place" seems to be the favorite. There is a definite pause after this, then follows an elaboration of all or parts of the Lord's

Prayer. Follows after that what I call the setting, that is, the artist calling attention to the physical situation of himself and the church. After the dramatic setting, the action begins.

There are certain rhythmic breaks throughout the prayer, and the church "bears him up" at every one of these. There is in the body of the prayer an accelerando passage where the audience takes no part. It would be like applauding in the middle of a solo at the Metropolitan. It is here that the artist comes forth. He adorns the prayer with every sparkle of earth, water and sky, and nobody wants to miss a syllable. He comes down from this height to a slower tempo and is borne up again. The last few sentences are unaccompanied, for here again one listens to the individual's closing peroration. Several may join in the final amen. The best figure that I can think of is that the prayer is an obligato over and above the harmony of the assembly.

CONVERSIONS AND VISIONS

The vision is a very definite part of Negro religion. It almost always accompanies conversion. It almost always accompanies the call to preach.

In the conversion the vision is sought. The individual goes forth into waste places and by fasting and prayer induces the vision. The place of retirement chosen is one most likely to have some emotional effect upon the seeker. The cemetery, to a people who fear the dead, is a most suggestive place to gain visions. The dense swamps with the possibility of bodily mishaps is another favorite.

Three days is the traditional period for seeking the vision. Usually the seeker is successful, but now and then he fails. Most seekers "come through religion" during revival meetings, but a number come after the meeting is closed.

Certain conversion visions have become traditional, but all sorts of variations occur, from the exceedingly frivolous to the most solemn. One "seeker" may go to a dismal swamp, the other to the privy house. The imagination may carry one to the last judgment and the rimbones of nothing, the vision of another may hobble him at the washing of collard greens. But in each case there is an unwillingness to believe—to accept the great good fortune too quickly. So God is asked for proof. One man told me that he refused to believe that he had truly been saved and said: "Now, Lord, if you have really saved my soul, I ask you to move a certain star from left to right." And the star shot across the heavens from the left hand to the right. But still he wouldn't believe. So he asked for the sun to shout and the sun shouted. He still didn't believe. So he asked for one more sign. But God had grown impatient with his doubtings and told him sharply that if he didn't believe without further proof that He'd send his soul to hell. At that, the man ran forth from his hiding and proclaimed a new-found savior.

In another case, a woman asked that a tree be moved and it stepped over ten feet, and then she asked for the star and God told her He had given her one sign and if she couldn't believe and trust Him for the balance He'd send her soul to torment.

Another woman asked for a windstorm and it came. She asked for the star to move and it did. She asked for the sun to shout and God grew angry and rebuked her like the others.

Still another woman fell under conviction in a cow lot and asked for a sign. "Now, Lord, if you done converted my soul, let dat cow low three times and I'll believe. A cow said, "Mooo-oo, moo-oo, moo-ooo-oo—and I knowed I had been converted and my soul set free."

Three is the holy number and the call to preach always comes three times. It is never answered until the third time. The man flees from the call, but is finallly brought to accept it. God punishes him by every kind of misfortune until he finally acknowledges himself beaten and makes known the call. Some preachers say the spirit whipped them from their heads to their heels. They have been too sore to get out of bed because they refused the call. This never ceased until the surrender. Sometimes God sends others to tell them they are chosen. But in every case the ministers refuse to believe the words of even these.

We see that in conversion the sinner is first made conscious of his guilt. This is followed by a period called "lyin' under conviction" which lasts for three days. After which Jesus converts the supplicant, and the supplicant refuses to believe without proof, and only gives in under threat of eternal damnation. He flees from this to open acknowledgment of God and salvation. First from the outside comes the accusation of sin. Then from within the man comes the consciousness of guilt, and the sufferer seeks relief from Heaven. When it is granted, it is at first doubted, but later accepted. We have a mixture of external and internal struggles.

The call to preach is altogether external. The vision seeks the man. Punishment follows if he does not heed the call, or until he answers.

In conversion, then, we have the cultural pattern of the person seeking the vision and inducing it by isolation and fasting. In the call to preach we have the involuntary vision—the call seeking the man.

COMING THROUGH RELIGION

I went out to pray in my back yard. I had done prayed and prayed but didn't know how to pray. I had done seen vision on top of vision, but still I wouldn't believe. Then I said: "Lord, let my head be a footstool for you." He says: "I plant my feet in the sea, follow after me. Your sins are forgiven and your soul set free. Go and tell the world what a kind of Savior you have found." I broke out the privy and went running and the voice kept following: "I set your feet on the rock of eternal ages; and the wind may blow and the storm may rise, but nothing shall frighten you from the shore."

I carried them messages.

"Jesus," "I am Jesus." "Father!" "I am the Father, and the Father in me." It just continued and He sent me to the unconverted. I had some more visions. In one of them I laid down and a white man come to me all dressed in white and he had me stretched out on de table and clipped my breath three times and the third time I rose and went to a church door and there was a weeping willow. There was a four-cornered garden and three more knelt with me in the four corners. And I had to pray, to send up a prayer.

The next vision I had a white woman says: "I am going home with you." I didn't want her to go. My house was not in order. Somebody stopped her. When I got home, a tall white man was standing at my door with a palmetto hat. I noticed he was pale-like. He was looking down on my steps. They was washed with redding.* He says: "I have cleaned your house. How do you like it?" I looked down on it and after he was gone I said: "I don't like that. It looks too much like blood." After I was converted it come to me about the blood and I knew it was Jesus, and my heart was struck with sorrow that to think I had been walking upon His precious blood all this time and didn't believe.

(Mrs. Susanna Springer)

I was a lad of a boy when I found Jesus sweet to my ever-dying soul. They was runnin p'tracted meetin and all my friends was gettin religion and joinin de church; but I never paid it no mind. I was hard. But I dont keer how hard you is, God kin reach you when He gits ready for you. One day, bout noon, it was de 9th day of June, 1886, when I was walkin in my sins, wallerin in my sins, dat He tetched me wid de tip of His finger and I fell right where I was and laid there for three long days and nights. I layed there racked in pain under sentence of death for my sins. And I walked over hell on a narrer foot log so I had to put one foot right in front de other, one foot right in front de other wid hell gapped wide open beneath my sin-loaded and slippery feet. And de hell hounds was barkin on my tracks and jus before dey rushed me into hell and judgment I cried: "Lawd, have mercy," and I crossed over safe. But still I wouldn't believe. Then I saw myself hangin over hell by one strand of hair and de flames of fire leapin up a thousand miles to swaller my soul and I cried: "Jesus, save my soul and I'll believe, I'll believe." Then I found myself on solid ground and a tall white man beckoned for me to come to him and I went, wrapped

---

*Brick dust is used in New Orleans to seam stone. It leaves them reddish.

in my guilt, and he 'nointed me wid de oil of salvation and healed all my wounds. Then I found myself layin on de ground under a scrub oak and I cried: "I believe, I believe." Then Christ spoke peace to my soul and de dungeon shook and my chains fell off, and I went shoutin in His name and praising Him. I put on de whole armor of faith and I speck to stay in de fiel till I die.

(Deacon Ernest Huffman)

First thing started me—it come to me dat I had to die. And worried me so I got talkin wid an old Christ man—about seventy years old. I wasn't but twentyone. And I started out from his instruction and I heered people say in my time dat de speerit would command you to de graveyard (to pray). And I ast de Lawd not to send me dere cause I wuz skeered uh de graveyard. But every answer I got commanded me to the graveyard and I didn't go. And de Lawd sent Death after me and when I knowed anything I was on my way to de graveyard. And when I got dere I fell. I fell right between two graves and I saw Him when He laid me upon a table in my vision. I was naked and He split me open. And there was two men there—one on each side of de table. I could hear de knives clicking in me, inside. And after dey got through wid me, they smother they hand over de wound and I wuz healed. And when I found myself I wuz standin naked beside de table and there was three lights burnin on de table. De one in de middle wuz de brightest. I wuzn't between de two graves no more. When I got up from between de two graves, I tracked my guide by de drops of blood. I could hear de blood dripping from Him before me. It said as it dropped: "Follow me." And I looked at de three lights and dey tole me to reach forth wid my right hand and grasp de brightest one and I did. It wuz shining like de Venus star. And they tole me it wuz to be my guidin star. I found myself before I left de table wid five white balls in each hand. "Them is the ten tablets I give you." And I put my hands to my breast and I put the balls inside me. Then He slapped something on my breast and said: "Go to yonder white house. You will find there one who will welcome you." An when I got to de steps I thowed my foot on de first step and de house rang and a lady come out and welcomed me in. And when I got inside, as far as mortal eye could behold, the robes was hanging level and touched my head as I passed under. Then I found myself robed in the color of gold. Then I commenced shouting. And when I commenced shouting I found myself leaving the graveyard. And He told me that was my robe for me bye and bye. In dat swamp where dat graveyard was there was catamounts and panters and wild beasts but not a one of 'em touched me and I laid there all night.

Now He tole me, He said: "You got the three witnesses. One is water, one is spirit, and one is blood. And these three correspond with the three in heben—Father, Son and Holy Ghost."

Now I ast Him about this lyin in sin and He give me a handful of seeds and He tole me to sow 'em in a bed and He tole me: "I want you to watch them seeds." The seeds come up about in places and He said: "Those seeds that come up, they died in the heart of the earth and quickened and come up and brought forth fruit. But those seeds that didn't come up, they died in the heart of the earth and rotted.

"And a soul that dies and quickens through my spirit they will live forever, but those that dont never pray, they are lost forever."

(Rev. Jessie Jefferson)

SHOUTING

There can be little doubt that shouting is a survival of the African "possession" by the gods. In Africa it is sacred to the priesthood or acolytes, in America it has become generalized. The implication is the same, however, it is a sign of special favor from the spirit that it chooses to drive out the individual consciousness temporarily and use the body for its expression.

In every case the person claims ignorance of his actions during the possession.

Broadly speaking, shouting is an emotional explosion, responsive to rhythm. It is called forth by: (1) sung rhythm; (2) spoken rhythm; (3) humming rhythm; (4) the foot-patting or hand-clapping that imitates very closely the tom-tom.

The more familiar the expression, the more likely to evoke response. For instance, "I am a soldier of the cross, a follower of the meek and lowly lamb. I want you all to know I am fighting under the blood-stained banner of King Jesus" is more likely to be amen-ed than any flourish a speaker might get off. Perhaps the reason for this is that the hearers can follow the flow of syllables without stirring the brain to grasp the sense. Perhaps it is the same urge that makes a child beg for the same story even though he knows it so well that he can correct his parents if a word is left out.

Shouting is a community thing. It thrives in concert. It is the first shout that is difficult for the preacher to arouse. After that one they are likely to sweep like fire over the church. This is easily understood, for the rhythm is increasing with each shouter who communicated his fervor to someone else.

It is absolutely individualistic. While there are general types of shouting, the shouter may mix the different styles to his liking, or he may express himself in some fashion never seen before.

Women shout more frequently than men. This is not surprising since it is generally conceded that women are more emotional than men.

The shouter always receives attention from the church. Members rush to the shouter and force him into a seat or support him as the case might be. Sometimes it is necessary to restrain him to prevent injury to either the shouter or the persons sitting nearest, or both. Sometimes the arms are swung with such violence that others are knocked down. Sometimes in the ecstacy the shouter climbs upon the pew and kicks violently away at all; sometimes in catalepsis he falls heavily upon the floor and might injure himself if not supported, or fall upon others and wound. Often the person injured takes offense, believing that the shouter was paying off a grudge. Unfortunately this is the case at times, but it is not usual.

There are two main types of shouters: (1) silent; (2) vocal. There is a sort of intermediary type where one stage is silent and the other vocal.

The silent type take with violent retching and twitching motions. Sometimes they remain seated, sometimes they jump up and down and fling the body about with great violence. Lips tightly pursed, eyes closed. The seizure ends by collapse.

The vocal type is the more frequent. There are all gradations from quiet weeping while seated, to the unrestrained screaming while leaping pews and running up and down the aisle. Some, unless restrained, run up into the pulpit and embrace the preacher. Some are taken with hysterical laughing spells.

The cases will illustrate the variations.

(1) During sermon. Cried "well, well" six times. Violent action for forty seconds. Collapsed and restored to her seat by members.

(2) During chant. Cried "Holy, holy! Great God A'mighty!" Arose and fell in cataleptic fit backwards over pew. Flinging of

92

arms with clenched fists, gradually subsiding to quiet collapse. Total time: two minutes.

(3) During pre-prayer humming chant. Short screams. Violent throwing of arms. Incoherent speech. Total time: one minute thirty seconds.

(4) During sermon. One violent shout as she stood erect: two seconds. Voiceless gestures for twenty-nine seconds. She suddenly resumed her seat and her attention to the words of the preacher.

(5) During sermon. One single loud scream: one and one-half seconds.

(6) During singing. Violent jumping up and down without voice. Pocket book cast away. Time: one minute forty seconds.

(7) During prayer. Screaming: one second. Violent shoulder-shaking, hat discarded: nineteen seconds.

(8) During sermon. Cataleptic. Stiffly back over the pew. Violent but voiceless for twenty seconds. Then arms stiff and outstretched, palms open stark and up. Colllapse. Time: three minutes.

(9) During sermon. Young girl. Running up and down the aisle: thirty seconds. Then silence and rush to the pulpit: fourteen seconds; prevented at the altar rail by deacon. Collapse in the deacon's arms and returned to seat. Total time: one minute fifteen seconds.

(10) During chant after prayer. Violent screams: twelve seconds. Scrambles upon pew and steps upon the back of pew still screaming: five seconds. Voiceless struggle with set teeth as three men attempt to restore her to seat. She is lifted horizontal but continues struggle: one minute forty-eight seconds. Decreasing violence, making ferocious faces: two minutes. Calm with heavy breathing: twenty-one seconds.

(11) During sermon. Man quietly weeping: nineteen seconds. Cried "Lawd! My soul is burning with hallow-ed fire!" Rises and turns round and round six times. Carried outside by the deacons.

(12) During sermon. Man jumping wildly up and down flat-footed crying "Hallelujah!": twenty-two seconds. Pulled back into his seat. Muscular twitching: one minute thirty-five seconds. Quiet weeping: one minute. Perfect calm.

THE SERMON

as heard by Zora Neale Hurston from
C. C. Lovelace, at Eau Gallie in Florida, May 3, 1929

(spoken)

"Our theme this morning is the wounds of Jesus. When the Father shall ask 'What are these wounds in thine hand?' He shall answer, 'Those are they with which I was wounded in the house of my friends.' (Zach, xiii. 6.)

"We read in the 53rd Chapter of Isaiah where He was wounded for our transgressions and bruised for our iniquities; and the apostle Peter affirms that His blood was spilt from be-. fore the foundation of the world.

"I have seen gamblers wounded. I have seen desperadoes wounded; thieves and robbers and every other kind of characters, law-breakers, and each one had a reason for his wounds. Some of them was unthoughtful, and some for being overbearing, some by the doctor's knife. But all wounds disfigures a person.

"Jesus was not unthoughtful. He was not overbearing. He was never a bully. He was never sick. He was never a criminal before the law and yet He was wounded. Now a man usually gets wounded in the midst of his enemies; but this man was wounded, says the text, in the house of His friends. It is not your enemies that harm you all the time. Watch that close friend, and every sin we commit is a wound to Jesus. The blues we play in our homes is a club to beat up Jesus; and these social card parties. . . ."

Jesus have always loved us from the foundation of the world.
When God
Stood out on the apex of His power
Before the hammers of creation
Fell upon the anvils of Time and hammered out the ribs
    of the earth
Before He made ropes
By the breath of fire
And set the boundaries of the ocean by gravity of His power
When God said, ha!
Let us make man
And the elders upon the altar cried, ha!
If you make man, ha!
He will sin.
God my master, ha!
Christ, yo' friend said
Father!! Ha-aa!
I am the teeth of Time
That comprehended de dust of de earth
And weighed de hills in scales
Painted de rainbow dat marks de end of de departing storm
Measured de seas in de holler of my hand
Held de elements in a unbroken chain of controllment.
De Moon, Ha!
Grabbed up de reins of de tides
And dragged a thousand seas behind her
As she walked around de throne—
Ah-h, please make man after me
But God said, No.
De stars bust out from their diamond sockets
And circled de glitterin throne cryin
A-aah! Make man after me

God said, No!
I'll make man in my own image, ha
I'll put him in de garden
And Jesus said, ha!
And if he sin,
I'll go his bond before yo mighty throne
Ah, He was yo friend
He made us all, ha!
Delegates to de judgment convention
Ah!
Faith hasnt got no eyes, but she's long-legged
But take de spy-glass of Faith
And look into dat upper room
When you are alone to yourself
When yo' heart is burnt with fire, ha!
When de blood is lopin thru yo veins
Make man, ha!
If he sin, I will redeem him
I'll break de chasm of hell
Where de fire's never quenched
I'll go into de grave
Where de worm never dies, Ah!
So God A'mighty, ha!
Got His stuff together
He dipped some water out of de mighty deep
He got Him a handful of dirt, ha!
From de foundation sills of de earth.
He seized a thimble full of breath, ha!
From de drums of de wind, ha!
God my master!
Now I'm ready to make man
Aa-aah!
Who shall I make him after? Ha!
Worlds within worlds begin to wheel and roll

De Sun, Ah!
Gethered up de fiery skirts of her garments
And wheeled around de throne, Ah!
Saying, Ah, make man after me, Ah!
God gazed upon the sun
And sent her back to her blood-red socket
And shook His head, ha!
Like de iron monasters (monsters) on de rail
Look into dat upper chamber, ha!
We notice at de supper table
As He gazed upon His friends, ha!
His eyes flowin wid tears, ha!
"My soul is exceedingly sorrowful unto death, ha!
For this night, ha!
One of you shall betray me, ha!
It were not a Roman officer, ha!
It were not a centurion soldier
But one of you
Who I have chosen my bosom friend
That sops in the dish with me shall betray me."
I want to draw a parable.
I see Jesus
Leaving heben with all of His grandeur
Disrobin Hisself of His matchless honor
Yieldin up de sceptre of revolvin worlds
Clothing Hisself in de garment of humanity
Coming into de world to rescue His friends
Two thousand years have went by on their rusty ankles
But with the eye of faith I can see Him
Look down from His high towers of elevation
I can hear Him when He walks about the golden streets
I can hear 'em ring under His footsteps
Sol me--e-e, Sol do
Sol me-e-e, Sol do

I can see Him step out upon the rim bones of nothing
Crying I am de way
De truth and de light
Ah!
God A'mighty!
I see Him grab de throttle
Of de well ordered train of mercy
I see kingdoms crush and crumble
Whilst de angels held de winds in de corner chambers
I see Him arrive on His earth
And walk de streets thirty and three years
Oh-h-hhh!
I see Him walking beside de sea of Galilee wid his disciples
This declaration gendered on His lips
"Let us go on the other side"
God A'mighty!
Dey entered de boat
Wid their oarus (oars) stuck in de back
Sails unfurled to de evenin breeze
And de ship was now sailin
As she reached de center of de lake
Jesus was 'sleep on a pillow in de rear of de boat
And de dynamic powers of nature become disturbed
And de mad winds broke de heads of de western drums
And fell down on de Lake of Galilee
And buried themselves behind de gallopin waves
And de white-caps marbilized themselves like an army
And walked out like soldiers goin to battle
And de zig-zag lightning
Licked out her fiery tongue
And de flying clouds
Threw their wings in the channels of the deep
And bedded de waters like a road-plow
And faced de current of de chargin billows

And de terrific bolts of thunder—they bust in de clouds
And de ship begin to reel and rock
God A'mighty!
And one of de disciples called Jesus
"Master!! Carest thou not that we perish?"
And he arose
And de storm was in its pitch
And de lightin played on His raiments as He stood on the
  prow of the boat
And placed His foot upon the neck of the storm
And spoke to the howlin winds
And de sea fell at His feet like a marble floor
And de thunders went back in their vault
Then He set down on de rim of de ship
And took de hooks of His power
And lifted de billows in His lap
And rocked de winds to sleep on His arm
And said, "Peace be still."
And de Bible says there was a calm.
I can see Him wid de eye of faith
When He went from Pilate's house
Wid the crown of 72 wounds upon His head
I can see Him as He mounted Calvary and hung upon de
  cross for our sins.
I can see-eee--ee
De mountains fall to their rocky knees when He cried
"My God, my God! Why hast thou forsaken me?"
The mountains fell to their rocky knees and trembled like
  a beast
From the stroke of the master's axe
One angel took the flinches of God's eternal power
And bled the veins of the earth
One angel that stood at the gate with a flaming sword
Was so well pleased with his power

Until he pierced the moon with his sword
And she ran down in blood
And de sun
Batted her fiery eyes and put on her judgment robe
And laid down in de cradle of eternity
And rocked herself into sleep and slumber.
He died until the great belt in the wheel of time
And de geological strata fell aloose
And a thousand angels rushed to de canopy of heben
With flamin swords in their hands
And placed their feet upon blue ether's bosom and looked
    back at de dazzlin throne
And de arc angels had veiled their faces
And de throne was draped in mournin
And de orchestra had struck silence for the space of half
    an hour
Angels had lifted their harps to de weepin willows
And God had looked off to-wards immensity
And blazin worlds fell off His teeth
And about that time Jesus groaned on de cross and said,
    "It is finished."
And then de chambers of hell explode
And de damnable spirits
Come up from de Sodomistic world and rushed into de
    smoky camps of eternal night
And cried "Woe! Woe! Woe!"
And then de Centurion cried out
"Surely this is the Son of God."
And about dat time
De angel of Justice unsheathed his flamin sword and
    ripped de veil of de temple
And de High Priest vacated his office
And then de sacrificial energy penetrated de mighty strata
And quickened de bones of de prophets

And they arose from their graves and walked about in de
    streets of Jerusalem.
I heard de whistle of de damnation train
Dat pulled out from Garden of Eden loaded wid cargo goin
    to hell
Ran at break-neck speed all de way thru de law
All de way thru de prophetic age
All de way thru de reign of kings and judges—
Plowed her way thru de Jordan—
And on her way to Calvary when she blew for de switch
Jesus stood out on her track like a rough-backed mountain
And she threw her cow-catcher in His side and His blood
    ditched de train,
He died for our sins.
Wounded in the house of His friends.
Thats where I got off de damnation train
And dats where you must get off, ha!
For in dat mor-ornin', ha!
To dat judgment convention, ha!
When de two trains of Time shall meet on de trestle
And wreck de burning axles of de unformed ether
And de mountains shall skip like lambs
When Jesus shall place one foot on de neck of de sea, ha!
One foot on dry land
When His chariot wheels shall be running hub-deep in fire
He shall take His friends thru the open bosom of a unclouded
    sky
And place in their hands de hosanna fan
And they shall stand round and round His beatific throne
And praise His name forever.
Amen.

THE SANCTIFIED CHURCH

The rise of the various groups of "saints" in America in the last twenty years is not the appearance of a new religion as has been reported. It is in fact the older forms of Negro religious expression asserting themselves against the new.

Frequently they are confused with the white "protest protestantism" known as Holy-Rollers. There are Negro Holy-Rollers, but they are very sparse compared to the other forms of sanctification. The two branches of the Sanctified Church are: (a) Church of God in Christ, (b) Saints of God in Christ. There is very little difference between the two except for the matter of administration.

The Sanctified Church is a protest against the high-brow tendency in Negro Protestant congregations as the Negroes gain more education and wealth. It is understandable that they take on the religious attitudes of the white man which are as a rule so staid and restrained that it seems unbearably dull to the more primitive Negro who associates the rhythm of sound and motion with religion. In fact, the Negro has not been christianized as extensively as is generally believed. The great masses are still standing before their pagan altars and calling old gods by a new name. As evidence of this, note the drum-like rhythm of all Negro spirituals. All Negro-made church music is dance-possible. The mode and the mood of the concert artists who do Negro spirituals is absolutely foreign to the Negro churches. It is a conservatory concept that has nothing to do with the actual rendition in the congregations who make the songs. They are twisted in concert from their barbaric rhythms into Gregorian chants and apocryphal appendages to Bach and Brahms. But go into the church and see the priest before the altar chanting his barbaric thunder-poem before the altar with the audience behaving something like a Greek chorus in that they "pick him up" on every telling point and emphasize it. That is called "bearing him up" and it is not done just any old way. The chant that breaks out from time to time must grow out of what has been said and done. "Whatever point he come out on, honey, you bear him up on it," Mama Jane told the writer. So that the service is really drama with music. And since music without motion is unnatural among Negroes there is always something that approaches dancing—in fact *IS* dancing—in such a ceremony. So the congregation is restored to its primitive altars under the new name of Christ. Then there is the expression known as "shouting" which is nothing more than a continuation of the African "Possession" by the gods. The gods possess the body of the worshipper and he or she is supposed to know nothing of their actions until the god decamps. This is still prevalent in most Negro protestant churches and is universal in the Sanctified churches. They protest against the more highbrow churches' efforts to stop it. It must be noted that the sermon in these churches is not the set thing that is in the other protestant churches. It is loose and formless and is in reality merely a framework upon which to hang more songs. Every opportunity to introduce a new rhythm is eagerly seized upon. The whole movement of the Sanctified Church is a rebirth of song-making! It has brought in a new era of spiritual-making.

These songs by their very beauty cross over from the little store-fronts and the like occupied by the "Saints" to the larger and more fashionable congregations and from there to the great world. These more conscious churchgoers, despising these humble tune-makers as they do always resist these songs as long as possible, but finally succumb to their charm. So that it is ridiculous to say that the spirituals are the Negro's "sorrow songs." For just as many are being made in this post-slavery period as ever were made in slavery as far as anyone can find out. At any rate the people who are now making spirituals are the same as those who made them in the past and not the self-conscious propagandist that our latter-day pity men would have us believe. They sang sorrowful phrases then as they do now because they sounded well and not because of the thought-content.

Examples of new spirituals that have become widely known:
1. HE IS A LION OF THE HOUSE OF DAVID
2. STAND BY ME
3. THIS LITTLE LIGHT I GOT
4. I WANT TWO WINGS
5. I'M GOING HOME ON THE MORNING TRAIN
6. I'M YOUR CHILD

There are some crude anthems made also among these singers.
1. O Lord, O Lord, let the words of my mouth, O Lord
   Let the words of my mouth, meditations of my heart
   Be accepted in thy sight, O Lord.

(From the Psalm. "Let the words of my mouth and the meditation of my heart be accepted in thy sight, O Lord.")

2. Beloved, beloved, now are we the sons of God
   And it doth not yet appear what we shall be
   But we know, but we know, but we know, but we know,
   When He shall appear, when He shall appear,
   When He shall appear, when He shall appear
   We shall be like Him, we shall be like Him
   We shall see Him as He is

(St. Paul: Beloved, now are we the sons of God but it does not yet appear what we shall be. But we know that when He shall appear we shall be like Him and we shall see Him as He is.)

The Saints, or the Sanctified Church is a revitalizing element in Negro music and religion. It is putting back into Negro religion those elements which were brought over from Africa and grafted onto Christianity as soon as the Negro came in contact with it, but which are being rooted out as the American Negro approaches white concepts. The people who make up the sanctified groups, while admiring the white brother in many ways think him ridiculous in church. They feel that the white man is too cut and dried and business-like to be of much use in a service. There is a well-distributed folk-tale depicting a white man praying in church that never fails to bring roars of laughter when it is told. The writer first found the story in Polk county but later found it all over the south.

THE WHITE MAN'S PRAYER

"It had been a long dry spell and everybody had done worried about the crops so they thought they had better hold a prayer-meeting about it and ask God for some rain. So they asked Brother John to send up the prayer because everybody said that he was really a good man if there was one in the county. So Brother John got down on his knees in the meeting and began to pray, and this is how he prayed:

"O Lahd (this pronunciation is always stressed and always brings a laugh). The first thing I want you to understand is that this is a white man talking to you. This aint no Nigger whooping and hollering for something and then dont know what to do with it after he gits it. This is a white man talking to you and I want you to pay me some attention. Now in the first place, Lahd, we would like a little rain. Its been powerful dry round here and we needs rain mighty bad. But dont come in no storm like you did last year. Come cam (calm) and gentle and water our crops. And now another thing, Lahd, don't let these Niggers be as sassy this coming year as they have in the past. That all, Lahd, AMEN."

The real, singing Negro derides the Negro who adopts the white man's religious ways in the same manner. They say of that type of preacher, "Why he dont preach at all. He just lectures."

And the way they say the word "lecture" make it sound like horse-stealing. "Why, he sound like a white man preaching." There is great respect for the white man as law-giver, banker, builder, and the like but the folk Negro do not crave his religion at all. They are not angry about it, they merely pity him because it is generally held that he just can't do any better that way. But the Negro who imitates the whites comes in for spitting scorn. So they let him have his big solemn church all to himself while they go on making their songs and music and dance motions to go along with it and shooting new life into American music. I say American music because it has long been established that the tunes from the street and church change places often. So they go on unknowingly influencing American music and enjoying themselves hugely while doing so in spite of the derision from the outside.

It is to be noted the strong sympathy between the white "saints" and the Negro ones. They attend each other's meetings frequently, and it is interesting to see the white saint attempting the same rhythms and movements. Often the white preacher preaches the sermon (in the Negro manner) and the Negroes carry on the singing. Even the definite African "Possession" attitudes of dancing mostly on one foot and stumbling about to a loose rhythm is attempted. These same steps can be seen in Haiti when a man or a woman is "mounted" by a loa, or spirit.